AND GO-MOKU

THE ORIENTAL BOARD GAMES

SECOND REVISED EDITION

BY EDWARD LASKER

DOVER PUBLICATIONS, INC.
NEW YORK • NEW YORK

This Dover edition, first published in 1960, is
a revised version of the work published in 1934 by
Alfred A. Knopf, to which has been added a new
Preface and chapter, "Advanced Strategy."

Library of Congress Catalog Card Number: 60-50074

Manufactured in the United States of America
Dover Publications, Inc.
180 Varick Street
New York, N. Y. 10014

PREFACE

TO DOVER EDITION

SINCE THE ORIGINAL EDITION of this book appeared in 1934, the number of Go enthusiasts in this country has increased at an accelerating pace. To no small extent this was due to the stimulus provided by visits of prominent Japanese who had happened to see my book and were delighted to learn that their national game was making friends in the United States. They sought out our players and engaged them in friendly games which actually proved to be most valuable lessons.

Among these visitors were Dr. Ichiro Hatoyama, who became Japan's Prime Minister; Mr. Juichi Tsushima, Minister of State, and incidentally President of the Japanese Go Association; Mr. Katsuro Ueda of the Finance Ministry; Mr. Tadashi Adachi, President of Radio Tokyo; and a number of other important persons from industry and the arts—impressive evidence of the fine type of mind to which the game of Go appeals. After returning to Japan, these men persuaded some of the leading masters of the game to come to this country for extended periods to teach our players. Thanks to their efforts a number of Americans now boast the master title, conferred on them by the Japanese Go Association.

The study of the visiting masters' technique made me realize the woeful inadequacy of the original version of this book. I was naturally anxious to revise it, embodying in it as much as possible of the masters' teachings. Dover Publications' readiness to bring out the new version was indeed a great satisfaction to me, as since the book went out of print I have had to disappoint an ever mounting number of *aficionados* of the game who inquired where they might obtain a copy of it.

Students looking for further Go literature will find a small bibliography at the end of the book.

January, 1960   E. L.
New York, New York

Go equipment is carried by many stores throughout the country which handle merchandise imported from Japan. In New York City a variety of Go boards and stones made of different materials may be purchased from:

Macy's Department Store, Broadway at 34th Street

Takashimaya, Inc., 509 Fifth Avenue

Miya, Inc., 373 Park Avenue South

Katagiri & Co., 224 East 59th Street.

English translations of Go books written by Japanese Go masters are obtainable from:

Takao Matsuda, 110 Sullivan Street, New York, N.Y. 10012

The American Go Association, G.P.O. Box 41, New York, N.Y. 10001.

The American Go Association is also in a position to furnish a monthly *Go Journal* published in Tokyo in English, as well as other Go literature.

American and Japanese Go players meet regularly (on Fridays, Saturdays, and Sundays) at the *New York Go Club,* on the sixth floor of the Nippon Club, 145 West 57th Street, New York. Addresses of other meeting places may be obtained from the American Go Association.

PREFACE

TO FIRST EDITION

OFF AND ON FOR TWENTY-FIVE YEARS I have flirted with the idea of writing a book on the Oriental games of Go and Go-Moku, but for obvious reasons I preferred to wait until the implements of these games were on the market.

I learned to play Go in 1907 while studying at the University of Berlin, where I had occasion to watch Japanese students in their leisure hours engage in the game with astounding perseverance and passion. At first I scoffed at their claim that Go was comparable in depth to our game of Chess. On second thought, however, I realized that my Occidental pride was quite unfounded, because Chess, after all, was also an Oriental game. I studied Go without prejudice and actually became one of its ardent apostles.

My friends to whom I showed the game—some of them Chess lovers and some addicted to cards—soon preferred it, like myself, to all other games they knew. When I left Germany in 1912, the knowledge of the game had spread considerably and an enthusiast in Dresden had started a monthly Go-magazine, which is still flourishing today.

In this country my experience was quite similar. Friends to whom I explained the game were fascinated by it, if they were at all of the type who play games occasionally. In fact, I saw it convert people who had always looked down upon any game as pure waste of time. An amusing example of this type was a busy executive of a large Chicago concern who had permitted me grudgingly to explain the game to him and his wife. When I met him a year later, he told me he had cursed the day he learned to play Go, because his inability to withstand its fascination irritated him beyond measure. It had almost become a ritual with him to play at least one game with his wife every night.

The reason for the strong fascination which the game exerts is not difficult to find. I know of no other game in which extreme simplicity of rules is coupled with such wealth of combinations. One can learn the rules of the game in less than five minutes; but—to quote an Oriental exaggeration—it takes thirty years to master it. It is too bad that this is not quite true. I believe that we remain interested in a game only as long as it mystifies us. As soon as we know all about it play becomes mechanical and boresome.

After learning the very few rules which govern the game and which are explained in Chapter I, anyone may start out to play immediately, without studying the chapters on elementary tactics and advanced strategy, and he will find a great deal of fun in the contest, no matter how badly he plays.

If he seeks a short cut to proficiency, however, a perusal of Chapters III and IV will answer better than hundreds of practice games, because they summarize the experience of centuries of master play.

There are, of course, many people who do not want to concentrate for any length of time when they play a game, and evidently their number is large in the Orient, too, for on the same board and with the same men which serve for the game of Go a much easier game, called Go-Moku, is widely played.

Several versions of the game of Go have been suggested, retaining its rules, but reducing the size of the board, in order to shorten the game and to make it more easily mastered. The disadvantage of such versions is that though they are quite useful in training the beginner in the proper handling of tactical encounters, they materially decrease the opportunity for large-scale strategic operations which are really the most fascinating part of the game. The smallest size of board permitting strategic planning of any appreciable scope is one of 13 x 13 lines. A booklet for beginners extensively treating play on this size board has been written by Gilbert Rosenthal, M.D., of Baltimore.

In the Orient, the strongest Go masters are found in Japan, though the present world champion, Lin Kai Ho, as well as his predecessor, Go Sei Gen, are Chinese. They emigrated to Japan at the invitation of the Japanese Go Association. The tremendous popularity of the game in Japan is strikingly illustrated by the fact that during match games for the National championship large Go boards can be seen on street corners in cities throughout the land, with crowds watching as every move is recorded, much in the manner of baseball score boards during the world series games in our country.

The fact that a large part of the Japanese population is capable of following with intense interest an abstract game such as Go shows their innate intelligence and culture. My Chicago friend who resented the irresistible attraction of Go said to me with good reason: "A nation which plays this game is to be reckoned with."

I am convinced that Go will gradually share with Chess the leading position among intellectual games in the Occident, just as it has reigned supreme in the Orient for the last three to four thousand years. As a matter of fact, Go has actually replaced Chess as the favorite pastime of a great many people who are familiar with both games, particularly mathematicians and physicists.

CONTENTS

INTRODUCTION
THE HISTORY OF THE GAME

OUTSIDE OF CHESS, Go[1] is the only game which has survived the trial of many centuries without any material change in its rules. It is three times as old as Chess, if we believe old Chinese sources, according to which the famous Chinese Emperor Shun, who reigned from 2255 until 2206 B.C., invented the game in order to strengthen the mental faculties of his son Shokin.

Another version ascribes the invention to U, a vassal of Emperor Ketsu, who is also said to have invented playing-cards. This version seems more likely because it makes the game five hundred years younger and because U was a vassal and not an emperor. One is inclined to believe that in those old days, too, emperors left it to others to invent things for them.

It is certain that in the tenth century B.C.—that is, thirteen hundred years after the time of Shun—the game of Go was well known in China, for several old Chinese works dating from that period mention the game in poems and allegories.

---

[1] The proper Japanese name of the game is Igo, but it is commonly called **Go**. In Chinese the name is Wei-Ki.

While it cannot be established from those very early references whether the ancient game was played exactly like the Go of today, the matchless simplicity of the rules of the game makes it unlikely that it went through several stages of development as did the game of Chess, the present form of which is only about four hundred years old.

The size of the Go board appears to have undergone changes until it was found that a board of 19 x 19 lines was best suited for the game, but these changes did not affect the character of the game in any way, and so we are really justified in saying that Go is the oldest game in the world—about four thousand years old.

The historical data given here are taken from a compilation made by the Japanese historian Miyoshi from Chinese literature. Miyoshi points to an interesting parallel with the history of Chess when recording the fact that the game of Go flourished most whenever the interest in art and literature was at a high point. Outstanding in this respect was the period in China from about A.D. 200 to 600.

In the records of those days a man by the name of Osan is mentioned who lived in the third century and astounded his contemporaries by playing over from memory a complete game of Go after it had been finished and all men removed from the board. How much in the course of time players' memory of Go positions has been strengthened is shown by the fact that today there are hundreds of players in Japan who can repeat a game move for move, often quite a long time after it has been played. In fact, it is customary for a teacher, after playing with a pupil, to repeat the whole game and criticize the pupil's moves.

In old Chinese books many stories are found which show the high esteem in which the game of Go was held. To relate only one of them: During the Tsin dynasty there lived a Prince by the name of Sha-an who fought a long war with his nephew Sha-gen, during which many thousands of soldiers were killed. Tired of this murderous fighting, they finally agreed to let the victory be decided by a game of Go which they played with each other.

Players of outstanding mastery were honoured by the title *Ki-sei* or *Ki-sen; Ki* being the Chinese word for Go, while *sei* means "saint," and *sen* "sorcerer living in the mountains."

The first books devoted entirely to the game of Go were written during the T'ang dynasty (618–906) and the Sung dynasty (960–1126). In that period the game flourished in China and there were many excellent players.

Go was not introduced into Japan until the year 754 of our era, when the Japanese Ambassador Kibidaijin brought it with him from China. This was under the reign of the Japanese Emperor Koken Tenno, when China was ruled by Hiuan Tsung.

At first the game remained confined to the nobles of Japan and made little progress. About a hundred years later a Japanese Prince went to China and engaged the best Chinese Go-player, Koshi-gen, as his teacher.

An anecdote which is told about this Prince tends to show, however, that even the best players of those days were very poor, measured by today's standards.

To honour the Prince the Chinese always let their best players oppose him, and, naturally, he always lost. At last, in order to avoid these continued defeats, the Prince conceived the idea of imitating each move of his opponent. He placed every man on the point located symmetrically opposite to the one his opponent had played, and in this way he won.

If his Chinese adversaries had really been good players, they could never have been bluffed by this strategy. All they would have had to do was to occupy the point in the centre of the board to which there is no corresponding symmetrical position.

For three hundred years the knowledge of the game in Japan did not extend beyond the court of Kioto. In fact, it must have been forbidden to play Go outside of the court, for Miyoshi relates that in the year 1084 the Prince of Dewa, Kiowara no Mahira, introduced the game secretly in Dewa and in Oshu, and that, from then on, the number of nobles who played it increased rapidly and soon caused it to spread to the wealthy classes among the people.

In the beginning of the thirteenth century the game was generally known and played passionately among the soldiers. From the famous generals of those days down to the common soldier everybody who went to war played Go. They carried the Go board and men with them, and when a battle was over they took out the board and continued to fight peacefully.

In the sixteenth and seventeenth centuries many monks, writers, and ordinary business men became famous through their outstanding ability at Go. They were invited to the courts of the daimios, either to play with them or merely to play for them so that onlookers could enjoy their beautiful games. This custom still prevails today. Friends of the game get together and invite two masters to play a game while they watch, and they follow the game with a patience and an absorption which, to the Occidental, is astounding. These gatherings might be compared with Chess matches played in our Chess clubs while the members look on, but in Japan the interest in the game extends into much wider circles, and the knowledge of the game really forms part of a higher education.

Early in the seventeenth century a number of players developed who far exceeded all others in strength and subtlety. The best among them was Honinbo Sancha, who had originally been a monk and who later obtained permission to form a Go school. He often played with the leading statesmen of his day, who liked to amuse themselves with the game in their leisure hours, and he accompanied them on their travels and to the wars and was present at many battles.

Later, when one of these statesmen, Tokugawa Iyeyasu, became the ruler of Japan, Honinbo Sancha was made the principal of a national Go academy, and the other outstanding players were made professors. Honinbo was given three hundred and fifty tsubo of land and received two hundred koku of rice every year, so that he was free from worry about his daily bread and could devote his time to training gifted pupils and developing the game.

These pupils soon outplayed the older players of the country, who lacked the training of the academy, and they became professional players. They either found employment at the courts of the daimios or travelled throughout the land, like the poets and fencing masters of those days, giving lessons and staying where they were well received.

Honinbo created the custom of ranking the professional masters according to their playing strength, the first rank being the lowest, the ninth rank the highest. This ranking system is still in force today. Nippon Kiin, The Japanese National Go Association, holds two great tournaments every year to bring the ranking up to date. The leading amateurs are also divided into nine classes. In their case the first rank is the highest, the ninth rank the lowest.

Among good players the one of higher rank will win fairly regularly. To equalize the chance to win, the weaker player, therefore, always receives a handicap. The game lends itself readily to a method of handicapping which has no parallel in Occidental games. The greater the difference in playing strength, the more moves the weaker player is permitted to make at the start before the stronger player places his first stone.

An amateur player of the first rank usually gives a two stone handicap to one of the second rank, three stones to one of the third rank, and so on. Among professional masters, however, the difference in playing strength between succeeding ranks is so small that a player cannot give a handicap of more than one stone for each three classes by which he outranks his opponent. A ninth rank master would let one of the eighth rank merely move first in two out of three games, and a seventh rank master would make the first move in every game. Similarly, a sixth rank master would get a two stone handicap in one out of three games, a fifth rank master in two out of three games, and a fourth rank master in every game. However, a ninth rank master is hardly ever paired with a player classed lower than fifth rank. Even a professional of the lowest rank can give an amateur of the highest rank a handicap of three stones. The same is true of games between professionals and amateurs who hold the "honorary master" degree sometimes bestowed on prominent persons.

In the 250 years of the Go Academy's life only nine players ever reached the ninth rank and another nine the eighth rank. There were quite a number of the seventh rank and many of the lower ranks.

Honinbo Sancha adopted his best pupil, who was then also called Honinbo and inherited the position of principal at the academy at the time of Honinbo Sancha's death. This manner of adoption was kept up even after the academy was discontinued in 1868, when the reign of the taikuns was overthrown. Thus the name of all Japanese Go champions was—and is still today—Honinbo. This name is reserved for Japanese nationals and was therefore not given to Go Sei Gen or Lin Kai Ho, the two Chinese masters who, however, are acknowledged to be world champions because they emerged victorious in competitions open to the strongest masters of all nations, including present and past Honinbos. There is little doubt that the older top-ranking masters will soon be overtaken by younger players. Just as in Chess, so many masters have reached a playing strength in Go which is only shades below that of the highest level, that physical stamina rather than superior strategy is apt to decide the outcome of hard fought tournament games. In modern Chess tournaments, sessions last five hours and unfinished games are adjourned until another day. In Go tournaments they often play ten hours a day or more, with only a short respite for lunch. After four or even three hours of continuous concentration, the brain of players in their forties or fifties begins to fatigue. This often results in elementary blunders in positions which they would easily have won had they not been tired out. Young players do not usually suffer from such attacks of Chess or Go blindness and for this reason practically dominate all tournaments today.

A number of leading Go masters of this generation have written books dealing with the advanced strategy of the game, and some of them have been translated into English. Most of the examples in Chapter IV have been taken from a book entitled *The Vital Points of Go* by Kaku Takagawa, a master of the ninth rank.

« 1 »

FUNDAMENTALS

THE GO BOARDS USED IN THE ORIENT are made of wood, usually between four and five inches thick, and supported by four feet, which make the whole board about eight inches high, convenient for players who squat on mats. More modern boards, intended to be placed on tables, are only about an inch or an inch and a half thick.

On the board 19 x 19 lines are drawn, parallel to the edges. The board does not form exactly a square, but is slightly oblong, the narrower sides facing the players. The horizontal lines are 29/32″ apart from each other and the vertical lines 27/32″.

The stones are not placed on the squares, as in Chess or Checkers, but on the points of intersection of the lines. There are 361 of these points all together, and each player has 181 stones, though rarely more than 125 to 150 are used in a game. The stones have the form of a convex lens about 7/8″ in diameter and ³⁄₃₂″ to ⅜″ thick in the centre. In Japan the black stones are usually made of slate, and the white stones of shells, the latter a shade larger than the former, and both a little too large for the space on the board, so that during the play they overlap here and there and lend a feeling of irregularity to the whole board which is enhanced still further by the careless manner in which the players place the stones on the points.

All this has perhaps grown out of the innate artistic sense of the Oriental, who is opposed to the monotony entailed in excessive regularity.

Cardboard is not a suitable material for Go boards. When a stone is grasped between the nail of the second finger and the tip of the third finger, as the Japanese do, and placed on the board with decision, a cheerful sound results on wood, but only a dull thud on cardboard.

In order to describe the points on the board in discussing moves and positions the algebraic method which is used in Chess is best suited. The vertical lines from the left to the right of the player of the black stones are named a, b, c, etc., to t, omitting the j, and the horizontal lines are numbered 1, 2, 3, etc., to 19, beginning from the side on which the player of the black stones sits.

The 4th, 10th, and 16th lines, as well as lines d, k, and q, are drawn somewhat heavier than the rest of the lines to facilitate orientation. The nine intersections of these lines, which according to the system of notation just explained would be d4, k4, q4, d10, k10, q10, d16, k16, and q16, are distinguished by small dots or circles, which the Japanese call stars, and which serve as handicap points.

The rules of
the game   The game starts on the vacant board. With Black beginning, the players alternately place one stone on any unoccupied point they choose. An exception is a case, discussed later on, which occurs a number of times in almost every game, and in which there is one point a player can occupy only under certain specified conditions.

[2]

Once placed, a man is never moved. On the Go board, motion takes the form of extending a man's position in one direction or another by placing additional men on points located in that direction.

The main objective of the players is to join their men gradually into groups surrounding as many *vacant* points as possible, and to do this in such a manner that, with proper play on both sides, hostile men placed in the surrounded territory cannot escape capture. A stone or a group of stones is captured and removed from the board by the opponent when the latter occupies the last vacant point directly adjoining that stone or group *on a line*.

A second objective of a player is the capture of as many hostile men as possible. In games between reasonably good players the number of men captured only very rarely comes anywhere near the number of vacant points surrounded.

The game is over when neither player can make a move that increases the size of this territory or the number of his prisoners. Each player then scores the number of vacant points he has surrounded, less the number of his men captured by the opponent. The larger score wins, though in master games it is sometimes agreed that Black, to offset the advantage the first move gives him, must score at least 5 points more than White to be considered the winner.

The weaker player always takes the Black stones. When receiving a handicap, he starts by placing the agreed number of stones on the handicap points in accordance with the convention described on page 79, and then White makes his first move.

Beginners often misinterpret the rules of play cited without an actual demonstration on the board. Their most frequent error is to consider stones firmly connected which are not adjoining on a line. Let us look at the position in Dia-

gram 1 between the lines e and m and the lines 2 and 6. We
see here a Black and a White army, the former being partly
surrounded by the latter. Neither the Black nor the White
men are completely united to chains. Black's group still lacks
a stone at either f4 or g3 and a stone at k3 or i2. White's army
still lacks connection at e4, at e6 or f5, at g5 or h6, and at
k5. Let us assume that both Black and White will be able
to carry out these connections in due course. Then the question still remains: are the unoccupied points which are surrounded by Black really Black's territory or are the Black
stones lost, thus making the points they enclose as well as the
points on which they themselves are located White's territory?

To decide this question we have to establish under what
conditions a group of stones is permanently safe from capture. This definition does not form part of the rules of the
game but follows automatically from their application, as
some of the examples discussed later on will elucidate.

The Diagram illustrates eight cases in which White on the
move could immediately effect a capture. In the lower left
corner he could remove Black's man by playing a2. On the
left edge he would capture the Black stone with a11, and
with e17 he would kill the man on e16. Likewise, the Black
stones extending from p10 to m12 would be removed when
White occupies n12, their last "breathing space" or "liberty,"
as such vacant points adjoining a group are called. g12 is the
only liberty the 8 men around that point have left. Therefore, g12 does not represent Black territory. It is in White's
hands, together with the 8 points which will be vacant after
Black's men are removed from the board. White can play
g12, although his man is completely surrounded on that spot,
only because in occupying it he is killing the surrounding

[4]

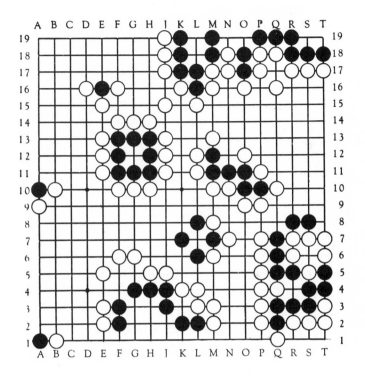

DIAGRAM I

group. The move would be illegal if Black still had another breathing space.

The positions around m7 and s5 illustrate the one exception *Ko* to the rule that a player may place a man on any vacant point of his choice. After White plays l7, capturing Black's man on m7, Black is not permitted to recapture White's stone immediately by playing back into m7. He must make a move at another part of the board before he returns to m7. A position of this type is called "Ko" and brings about the most interesting situations.

It is evident that unless Black makes a threat which White must answer in order not to lose more than he would gain by filling in the Ko at m7, his intervening move would not affect the Ko situation. If that move forces a reply on the part of White, however, Black will be able to recapture at m7 on the following move. White, again, will have to invent a threat which Black must answer before he can capture Black's man on m7 for the second time, and so on. Sometimes these Ko fights extend through a series of twenty or thirty moves and decide the outcome of the game.

Though this statement will not be clear until it is illustrated later on by an actual game, an inkling of the possibilities entailed in Ko situations will be conveyed by the position on the right side of Diagram 1. It is Black's move. White threatens to play r4, capturing seven Black men. Black cannot save these men by playing himself into r4, because White would reply q8, killing twelve men. Black will therefore play s6 and take White's man s5, at the same time attacking the five White men around s6. White cannot save these by playing t8, because Black would capture the group with t9. Thus White must invent a threat at another part of the board, important enough for Black to answer, and then he can recapture on s5, again attacking the seven Black men. Whether White wins these seven men or Black wins the six White men will depend upon who has more threats available to him elsewhere.

In the position shown in the upper part of Diagram 1 White threatens to play o19, which would not merely capture two men, but would separate Black's army into two groups. As we will see later, these groups could avoid getting captured only

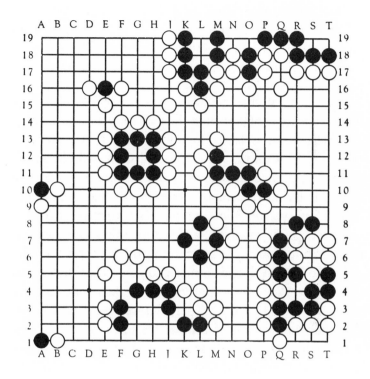

DIAGRAM I

when connected with each other. Black can ensure that connection by playing 1.n19, because after White replies 2.019,
taking two prisoners, Black recaptures with 3.018, taking one,
and if at any time White attacks the stone on 018 with 017, Black
can fill at 019, linking his groups solidly.

After White has played 019, Black is permitted to recap-

[7]

ture immediately, because this is not a case of Ko, inasmuch as White has captured more than one stone. If a White man were located on o17 instead of a Black one, so that White would take only one man by playing at o19, Black could not recapture until he had played a move elsewhere. In other words, the life of his army would then depend upon the outcome of a Ko fight.

In such a fight the players must carefully calculate how many points are at stake. Only then are they in a position to decide whether it is better to fill the Ko or to answer the opponent's threat. In the present case Black would lose fifteen men if White filled the Ko, and White would increase his territory by the fifteen points vacated by the captured stones, plus the four vacant points within Black's group. The total number of points involved is therefore thirty-four, less the number White would lose by ignoring Black's threat and filling the Ko instead. Let us assume, for argument's sake, that his net gain would be eighteen points. Before making his decision he would scan the positions on the board to see whether he has a threat of comparable size available to him. If so, he will defend himself against Black's threat and let him recapture in the Ko, whereupon Black will be guided by similar considerations on his next turn.

The beginner rarely realizes that a Ko threat need not necessarily involve the capture of a hostile group. It may instead merely prepare an invasion of territory which must be warded off to avoid a greater loss than at stake in the Ko. Diagram 2 will illustrate this point. Black has just captured in the Ko at d16. The stake is rather sizeable; for if Black could fill the Ko at c16, he would seal off about ten points in the corner, with good prospects of increasing this territory considerably

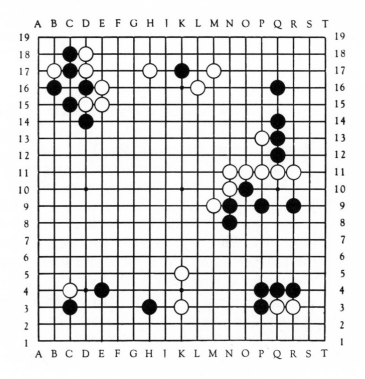

DIAGRAM 2

by expansion toward line k. If White wins the Ko, however, he will be able either to ruin Black's corner by playing b18 and capturing the men on c17 and c18, or to break into the territory on the side with c14, which would attack the man on c15.

White has excellent Ko threats of the territorial type at his disposal. He could invade Black's prospective territory on the upper right, for example, by playing r17. This would threaten q17 and incidentally promise a good chance of surrounding Black's men on line q completely. Or he could play p2, threatening to continue with o2 and n2 or m3, thus forming a chain connecting his three men on the third line and taking a territory of a good many points away from Black.

Let us now discuss a number of typical situations with which every beginner must be familiar to avoid sudden fatal losses.

In Diagram 3 the Black men on d3, d4, c5, and b6 partly surround the corner territory, while the White men on e3, e4, g5, h3, and h4 partly surround territory between the lines e and h. If Black plays 1.e2 and White replies 2.f2, the life of the Black man on e2 is threatened. For if Black makes a move on some other part of the board to which White need not answer immediately, White could continue with 4.d2, attacking e2 directly, and 5.e1 will not save Black because after 6.d1 and 7.f1 White captures the three Black men by 8.g1.

This is a very important play to remember, as it recurs many times in every game, owing to the fact that the opposing armies, in their desire to wall off territory within their lines, almost always extend these lines toward the edge of the board as far as the third line and frequently attempt to encroach upon the territory of the adversary by an advance in the second lines as just illustrated.

Sh'cho   The danger of capture by the method shown in this example always exists when a group of men has only two adjoining vacant points connected to it. In Diagram 3 the White group l13, l14, m13, for instance, would be lost if Black played 1.n13, occupying one of the two vacant points adjacent to the White group and threatening to kill the group with m12. For if White tries to save himself by 2.m12, Black plays 3.m11, again leaving only one point of escape for White. After 4.n12

[10]

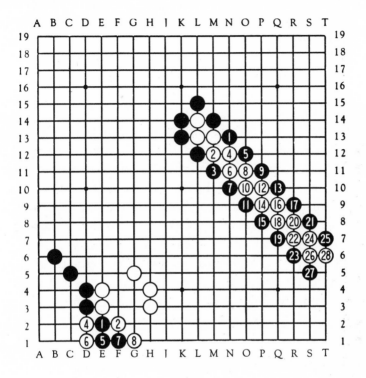

DIAGRAM 3

and 5.o12, 6.n11; 7.n10, 8.o11; 9.p11, etc., as indicated in the diagram, the White chain finally reaches the edge of the board, from where there is no further escape. After 26.s6, 27.s5, and 28.t6 Black kills the whole White army with 29.t5.

The play illustrated in the last two examples is called Sh'cho (the ladder). This method of attack must never be used if the ladder of the defending player zigzags toward a stone of his own. If a White man had been standing on q9, for instance, Black's move 15.p8 would leave White two open points in his chain instead of only one, so that he would have time to play 16.n14 or o13 or any one of several other moves available which attack two of Black's men simultaneously, winning one of them and providing an avenue of escape for the whole White army.

Another type of constellation in which the ladder attack cannot be employed is illustrated on the lower left of Diagram 4. If Black attacks with 1.f7, 2.e7; 3.e8, White escapes with 4.d7, because this move attacks Black's man d6. If no White stone had been standing on d5, Black would have won the White group if we disregard the men on lines 9, 10, and 11.

Similarly, Black cannot succeed by attacking with 1.e7, 2.f7; 3.f8, 4.g7; 5.h7, 6.g8; 7.g9, because White escapes with 8.h8 through attack on the Black man h7, who is threatened through co-operation with the White man on h6.

If Black played 1.d7, which does not directly attack the White group, White would have to make a defensive move all the same, because Black threatens 3.f7, and after 4.e7 Black would capture the White men by e8.

Along the edge of the Diagram 4 a number of errors are illustrated which every beginner makes frequently. Instead of playing a10 in answer to White's c10 Black should have connected at b11, or he should have played a11 or b12 in order to prevent White's b11 which, in the position of the diagram, wins two Black men. To play a16 instead of a15 or b15 is a very similar mistake. White does not protect the man on a17 which is attacked, but continues with b15 and wins the three Black men. Black's man i18 is lost through·White's k18, and the man on m19 is lost through White's n19 or l19. Again,

[12]

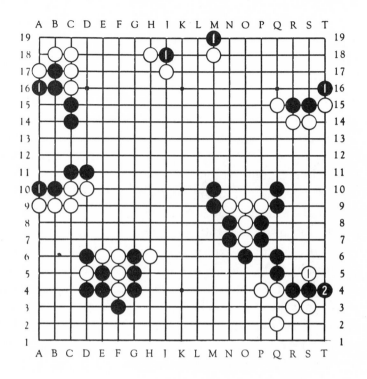

DIAGRAM 4

White need not protect his man on t15 when Black attacks with t16, but he can win Black's man through s16, because if Black takes White's man with t14, White continues with r16; and connecting at t15 does not save Black's men, since White would win them all through t13. Similarly Black should not have answered White's s5 with t4, but he should have connected at r5, for White can now win the three Black men through r5.

Around o9 a white group is shown which cannot escape capture. The method of capturing it should be studied carefully.

It is evident that White can neither escape with n10 nor o10 nor p10, because Black would place a man correspondingly on the eleventh line and enclose White from the top.

It is also easily seen that neither n11 nor p11 will help White, because Black answers n10 or p10 respectively and completes the enclosure from the top.

However, White can apparently save himself by starting with o11, threatening to connect on the next move with o10 and to run away into the open. This plan can only be met by Black's playing a man on o10 himself. White can attack this man by 3.n10, and if Black defended him with p10, White would indeed be safe through connection at n11. But Black plays 4.n11 himself, sacrificing the stone at o10, and after White takes him with 5.p10, Black continues 6.p11, threatening to take seven men by playing again into o10; and 7.o10 does not save White, because Black replies 8.o12, capturing the whole group of nine men.

Seki   Not infrequently positions occur in which an army is safe although it has only two vacant points adjacent to its men, because the opposing army which surrounds it depends upon the same vacant points for its own life.

The position in the lower left of Diagram 5 is an example. The eleven White men which are surrounded by Black have only the points a2 and b2 open, but Black cannot attack the group by occupying either one of these two points because White would occupy the other, killing the six Black men by taking the last adjoining vacant point away from them.

[14]

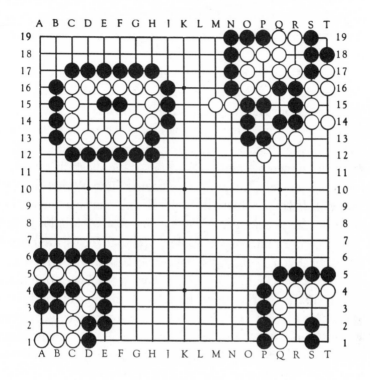

DIAGRAM 5

Neither can White attack the Black men by playing either a2, or b2, because Black would occupy the last vacant point and kill the twelve White stones.

A position of this type is called "Seki." It occurs more frequently in a form in which the two vacant points are not adjoining, but separated as in the position in the upper right of the diagram. White cannot attack the Black men in the corner with r18, because Black would reply p17, capturing eleven men. Neither can Black attack the White group with r18, because White would capture the attacking men with t19.

Of course, if later on in the game White should succeed in capturing the Black chain extending from n16 to p19, which is cut off from the rest of the Black army by the White men at n15 and o16, he would thereby relieve the Seki and he would also win the Black men in the corner.

In the upper left and lower right of the diagram two more examples of Seki are given. No matter how White plays, he cannot kill the intruders if Black replies correctly.

Apart from Seki there is only one type of position which is not conquerable, and it is this type that forms the basis of all tactical considerations on the board. Diagram 6 shows various examples of it. If in the position in the lower right-hand corner Black has the move, he can save his partly surrounded group by playing s1; for in order to capture the Black men, White would have to occupy r1 and t1, the two remaining vacant points connected to Black's group, and he can never accomplish this because a man placed on either one of these two points would be automatically dead since he would be completely surrounded by the enemy.

If it were White's move, he would win the Black group by playing s1, with the threat to continue with r1 and t1. True enough, after he plays r1, Black can capture the two men on s1 and r1 by playing t1. But then there are only two adjoining vacant spots left in Black's group instead of the original three. White again plays a man at s1, threatening to capture all six Black men by adding a man on r1. Black can stave the end off only another move. He can capture White's man by

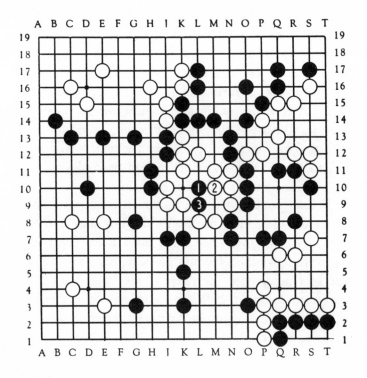

DIAGRAM 6

playing r1 himself. But this reduces the Black army to a single vacant point, and White, in occupying s1 for the third time, kills the seven Black men.

From this example we learn that an army, to be safe, must *Me** be able to form at least two *separate* breathing spaces. These are called the "eyes" of the army, "Me" in Japanese.

*Pronounced *meh*.   [17]

Groups of fair size which are not yet closely contacted by the enemy—like White's groups on the left and lower right, and Black's groups with the exception of the corner position just discussed—never have any difficulties in forming Me when defended early enough against invasion. When groups are already more or less encircled, like White's group on the upper right, it pays to form eyes at the first opportunity, even if this could be done readily at any time the opponent tries an invasion. Otherwise they offer welcome opportunities for Ko threats. Thus, in the diagrammed position, White would do well to play o13 or s14, even though he could still form Me after Black occupies one of these points.

The White group in the center, which is cut off from its friends in the upper left by Black's diagonal cut at i13-k14, can no longer form Me after Black plays 1.l10. The attempt to do so with 2.m10 fails because Black replies 3.m10, occupying the spot needed for the purpose. He could then not be stopped from killing the White group in the manner discussed in connection with the lower right corner (See also Diagram 12, center).

The outer liberties of White's group are in contact also with Black stones, and none of them can therefore be completely encircled by White so as to form an eye.

False Me   Diagram 7 shows positions in which armies containing two or more separate vacant points are lost all the same, because some vacant points are "false Me"—that is, eyes which can be closed by an attack on part of the men forming them.

In the lower left the White group contains the eyes a1 and b2; but if it is Black's move, he can play c1, thereby attacking c2, and after White fills b2 there is only one eye left and the group is dead; by playing a4 White would form only another false Me, since Black can attack a4 with a man on a5.

The White group on the right side of the diagram con-

[18]

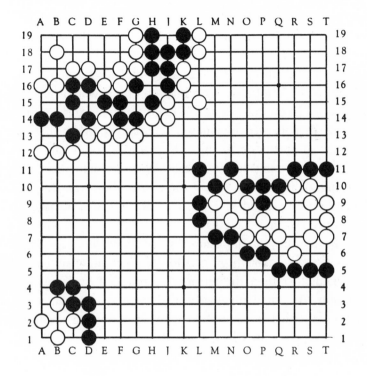

DIAGRAM 7

tains apparently three eyes, one on n9, one on o8, and one around r8; however, Black on the move plays r8, reducing the vacant points in this territory to one eye, as demonstrated in connection with Diagram 6. The White army is then lost because n9 is a false eye owing to the attack on n10 and after n9 and m8 are filled by either White or Black the whole left wing of White's army is attacked and could only be saved by

White filling o8 whereupon White's group contains only the one eye around r8 and cannot evade capture.

The Black army in the upper left apparently contains five eyes, but only the one in i19 is genuine. If Black plays 1. b13, threatening to continue with b15, which would form a secure eye on c14, White answers 2.b15, destroying this eye, for after a13 and a15 are filled in, the left wing of Black's group would be captured by White placing a man on c14. It would not help Black to fill in on c14, because White by playing d15 captures all Black men located on lines a, b, c, and d. After that the Black group on lines e, f, and g is attacked, and it cannot be saved by connecting at g15, because White would reply h16, capturing all Black men except those located on h17, h18, and h19 and on lines i and k. These men are lost, too, because i19 is the only eye they have left.

A careful study of the examples illustrated in Diagrams 4, 5, 6, and 7 will enable beginners to tell when an army is alive and when, therefore, the territory surrounded by it is in its possession. As stated previously, the game is over when this question is settled in connection with all groups on the board and all territories on which they border.

Let us analyse an actual case. The position of Diagram 8 resulted in a game during which White had taken 17 prisoners, and Black had taken 8. The game is over because there is no vacant point on the board which does not clearly belong either to White or to Black, except f8, l6, and o15, which are located between the Black and White armies, in no man's *Dame** land. These points, which are called "Dame," are filled in by either White or Black.

It is evident that the territory on the right between the eighth and fourteenth line is in White's power, also the territory on the lower left between lines a and c and on the upper

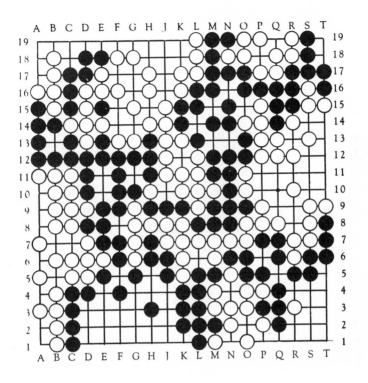

DIAGRAM 8

left between lines a and k and 14 and 19. The seven Black men in this territory are obviously lost because there is no room for them to form Me. The three Black men on h9, i9, and k9 are also lost, because the attempt to save them by capturing the White man on h10 with i10 fails, since White simply plays back into h10, taking all four Black men.

The small White group on the upper right is safe, as it contains two Me. The group on the lower right, however, between the first and the fifth lines, is dead because it contains only one Me, on o2, the eyes on n1 and n4 being false.

After removing the ten dead Black men from the board White has a total of 27 prisoners, while the twelve White men removed from the lower right swell Black's number of prisoners to 20.

Black has very little territory outside of the large space on the lower edge; just three points in the upper left quadrant and seven in the upper right.

Scoring To determine who has won the game, the vacant points surrounded by each player would have to be counted, and the number of White prisoners would have to be deducted from White's territory, and the number of Black prisoners from Black's. To simplify the counting the prisoners are simply filled into the territory of the army of the same color, which saves the work of actually counting and subtracting their number. Each player counts and fills in the space of his opponent. In this case Black would use his 20 prisoners to fill in the five White points in the centre, the two in the upper right, the six on the 12th, 13th, and 14th lines, and the seven on the 8th, 9th, and 10th lines on the right side. White would use his 27 prisoners to fill in the seven Black points in the upper right quadrant, the three points in the upper left quadrant, and the seventeen points on the 4th, 5th, and 6th lines.

Though it would not take very long now to count the remaining vacant points, the task is further simplified by arranging the men within their territory in such manner as to leave rows of five or ten points wherever possible.

Thus, White would take the three men from a3, a5, and a7 and place them on b5, b7, and c7, leaving just a row of

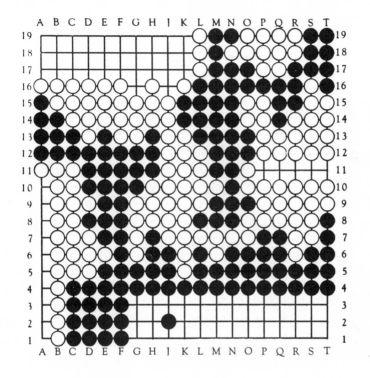

DIAGRAM 9

ten points on the left edge. The right side requires no rearrangement, since there is just a row of five points open. In the upper left quadrant the White men on b17 and b18 would be transferred to c15 and c16. The men on e17, f18, g18, h17, and k17 would be used to fill up the vacant points on the 14th and 15th rows, and the White territory is then easily counted

[23]

as 32 points, three rows of ten each and two points over in the 16th line. The total White territory is thus 32 plus 10 plus 5, or 47 points.

Black would take the ten men which are scattered on the 1st, 2nd, and 3rd rows and place them in the lines d, e, and f, leaving one man over, which has to be deducted from the remaining territory of 3 x 13 or 39 points. This gives Black a total of 38 points, so that he loses by 9 points.

Diagram 9 shows the picture which presents itself after the arrangement of the men as above described. It would, of course, have been permissible to rearrange them in any other fashion which occurred to the players as the quickest way to arrive at the result.

Beginners will find that, owing to the many bad mistakes they make, which often lead to the loss of fairly large armies, the difference in their scores is frequently very large, running up as high as fifty or even a hundred points. In Japan the score among players of about the same strength rarely differs by more than seven or eight points, and if the difference is evidently greater than ten or twelve points the player who is at the disadvantage resigns the game without actually finishing it.

Oriental players count the score fairly accurately during the game, as soon as the end game stage is reached—that is, the stage in which only the walling off of the territories has to be completed which the armies have more or less clearly defined in their encounter. Beginners usually do not know whether they have won or lost the game until they actually finish it and go through the counting as above illustrated.

« 2 »
ELEMENTARY TACTICS

ALTHOUGH THE RULES AND EXAMPLES given in the first chapter are sufficient to enable anyone to play the game of Go correctly, it would take the beginner a long time to find out empirically even the most common tactical manœuvres which the experienced player employs to gain an advantage, to say nothing of the more subtle strategic plays which distinguish master practice from the average game.

Owing to the size of the board the number of possible combinations is, of course, so vast that it would be idle to attempt giving an exhaustive analysis of these possibilities. However, we can study types of combinations which often recur with the same idea as a basis, though always varied in actual execution, and in this way we can arrive much more rapidly at a real understanding of the finer points of the game than by mere practical experience.

Usually beginners do not like to choose this path. They want to play a game as soon as they have learned the rules. The result, of course, is nothing remotely resembling the real game of Go. All the same, these fantastic attempts are not entirely useless, for they accustom the eye of the player to some of the most elementary traps and constellations and they enable him to foresee such traps the next time they are threatened.

Traps and sacrifices What confounds the beginner more than any other form of combinations are traps which involve the sacrifice of a man or a whole group of men. Such sacrifices, naturally, are offered only where their acceptance leads to a greater loss for the enemy. A simple type of sacrifice has already been discussed in connection with Diagrams 4 and 6. The idea is almost always the same—namely, to force the opponent to occupy, in capturing the sacrificed man, a place which cuts down the number of vacant points a defending army comprises within its territory. Diagram 10 illustrates a typical case. White's men in the left corner are pressed by Black, but at the same time they press themselves on Black's men in lines b, c, and d. It is Black's move and it looks as if he will lose his men because they have only three more vacant points adjoining while White's men have four, since Black cannot play a5 before making this approach safe through a6. This preliminary move White would answer with a2, leaving the points a1, b1, c2 and a5 open, while Black has only the points c2, d1, and e2 left. Black cannot gain more freedom by extending with e2, because White would confine him with f2, again keeping the number of open points in Black's chain down to three, and no matter how Black continues, he is bound to lose. For instance: 1.a6, 2.a2, 3.e2, 4.f2, 5.c2, 6.e1, 7.b1, 8.d1, and the Black men are captured on the next move.

However, Black can turn the tables by placing his first man at a2. White must accept this sacrifice, because otherwise Black captures the White group with a5. After 2.a1 the open points adjoining White's chain are reduced by one, and now Black wins by 3.a6, 4.e2, 5.a5, threatening to take on a2, for after 6.a2, 7.c2, White has only one point open, while Black has two.

[26]

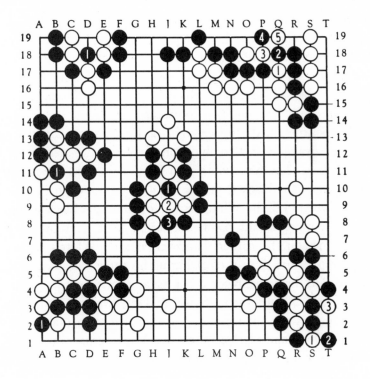

DIAGRAM 10

The position in the lower right-hand corner illustrates a similar manœuvre by which White saves his group, although the Black men in lines p and q can apparently secure more connections to vacant points by q1, s1, and t3 than White has at his disposal.

Black would indeed emerge victorious if White attacked

him with 1.p2, 2. s1, 3. p3, 4. q1, etc. However, White plays first s1, and after 2.t1 captures the sacrificed man, he gives up another man with 3.t3, so that after 4.t2, 5.p2, 6.s1, 7.p3, 8.q1, 9.p1 Black cannot save his group by filling in at t3, because White would capture it with 10.t5. In other words, White by his sacrifices, has reduced the vacant points adjoining Black's chain to the same number which he has himself, and since he moves first, he is the first to capture.

The position in the upper right of Diagram 10 is a more complex example of a combination involving the sacrifice of several men. The four white men from s16 to s19 appear to be lost, since the Black men r16, r17, and r18 can connect with p17 in time to kill the White man on o18, and the Black group has then more vacant points connected to it than the four White men in the corner. However, if after White's 1. q17 Black replies q18 instead of giving up his three men with p18, White wins the whole Black group as far as m18, by continuing with 3. p18, 4. p19; 5. q19, 6. o19 (taking two men); 7. p18, 8. o18 (takes one man); 9. r19, p18; 11.m19, n19 (takes one man); 13. p16, and Black cannot prevent the capture of his fourteen men because 14. m19 would be answered by 15. k19, taking sixteen men.

This combination may appear quite deep and difficult, but it is really nothing but an elaboration of the simple case illustrated in the centre of Diagram 10, in which Black kills the connection between the lower and upper five White men by first sacrificing a man on i10. After White has captured this man with i9 Black attacks with i8, and White cannot defend by filling at i10 because Black would capture nine White men with i13.

The type of combinations discussed in connection with the positions of Diagram 10 recurs frequently in every game and

[28]

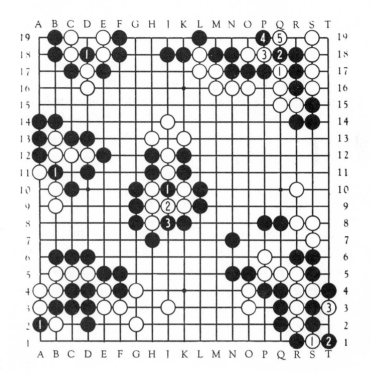

DIAGRAM 10

always arises when two groups are not solidly connected on straight lines, but permit a cut where a diagonal connection exists. Probably the simplest form of such a cut is shown in the two positions in the upper left of the diagram. White on the move could connect the six men in the corner by playing d18. But if it is Black's move, he plays d18 himself, and after White takes this man, Black re-enters the same point and captures five men.

Similarly, White, on the move, could connect seven men by playing b11, while Black on the move would capture part of White's men by first sacrificing a man on b11 and re-entering that point if White replies c11, taking Black's men.

In all combinations shown up to now one or more men were sacrificed in order to reduce the number of vacant points in the adversary's territory. We will now illustrate cases typical of a different kind of sacrifice, in which the object is to gain a "tempo" for an attack in another direction. This kind of attack also occurs frequently in every game and must therefore be thoroughly understood.

Diagram 11 offers some instructive examples. In the lower left corner Black offers the sacrifice of a man at e2, a common method employed to break the link between a lone man on the second line with a man on the third. White must not accept the sacrifice, for after 2.f2 Black would play 3.c2, forcing White to protect d2 by either capturing the man on e2 or playing d1, and then Black would strengthen his man by 5.b2 and he would win the two White men on c3 and c4, since they have only two vacant points connected to them, while the two Black men have three.

Instead, White must answer Black's 1.e2 with 2.b2. This threatens f2, and after Black destroys the prospective eye on c2 with 3.d1, and in reply to 4.c2 plays 5.f2 himself, White proceeds to make his group safe with 6.b5, 7.b6, 8.b7, 9.a5, which secures eyes at b4 and a2 or a1.

A subtle sacrifice of a man in order to gain a decisive tempo is the key to the manoeuvre with which White saves his four men on lines b and c and the three men on line 18 in the position at the upper left of the Diagram. Black threatens to

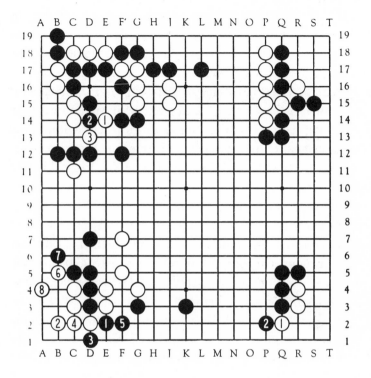

DIAGRAM II

kill the three men in three moves. White cannot play 1.c19
to catch Black's two men in the corner with a18 and thereby
save his own men, because 2.e19 would leave White with only
one liberty as against the two liberties of Black. Neither can
White start with 1.a18, because Black would again reply
2.e19 so that White cannot continue with c19 as Black's reply

d19 would kill the White men. 3.a19 would, of course, be impossible because of 4.a17, killing two men.

Thus, the chance for White to live lies in an attempt to capture the four Black men on c16, c17, d17, and e17 which keep his two groups apart. Failing in this, he would also lose his four men on the left because he would not have room for two Me. For example, if he started with 1.a17, threatening to catch Black's two men in the corner with a18 and a19 and thus forcing 2.e19 or c19, he could form an eye with 3.a15; but Black would stop him from making a second eye with 4.b14. Neither would 1.b13 work, because Black would play 2.a17 or a15.

White would accomplish nothing by attacking Black's group of four men with 1.e16. After 2.d16 they would connect either with the stones on the fourteenth or those on the twelfth line, depending upon whether White continues with 3.d14 or c15. Nor would 1.e15 have any success. Black would reply d14 and again safely connect his men.

The only way in which White can prevent this connection is by starting with 1.e14. Now, if Black plays 2.d14, White caps this stone with 3.d13, although this permits the double attack 4.e13. Then, after 5.e15, Black cannot connect at d16 because White would capture seven men by occupying e16. The best he could do would be to take White's man on d13 with 6.c13, giving up the four men which White then attacks with 7.e16 and which cannot be connected at d16 because the Black group of seven men would have only one liberty left which White can occupy.

Black would fare no better when answering White's diagrammed third move with 4.e15, attacking the stone on e14. White would sacrifice it with 5.f15, attacking in turn the man on f16. Black could then connect neither on e16 nor on d16

[32]

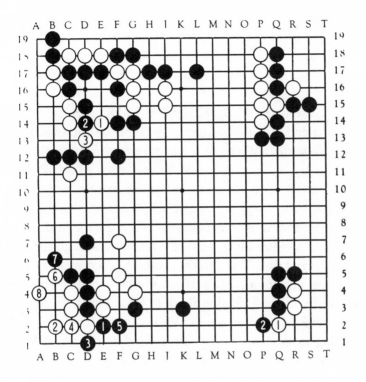

DIAGRAM II

because his whole group of ten men would have only one liberty and White would capture them on his next move. Black's only reply would be 6.e13, capturing the man on e14, and White would continue with e16, taking one man and winning the other four which the move attacks, for again Black could not connect on d16 as this would leave his whole group with only one breathing space at e14 which White could occupy.

[33]

To foresee clearly the consequences of the different moves White must consider in the diagrammed position would be no easy task even for an experienced player. It certainly could not be expected of a beginner. But playing several times through the variations analyzed above would prove very useful to him by keeping him alert to the possibility of similar combinations in his own games.

The position in the upper right of the Diagram might occur near the end of a game, when only points on the edge remain to be contested. White does not threaten to catch the three men on line q, as 1.r17 would be met with 2.r18 and White would lose his two intruders. But unless Black settles the frontier line with 1.p19, o19; 3.q19, which threatens o18, forcing White to answer at that point, and then guards himself with r17, he would lose all of his corner territory through the attack 1.s17!, r17; 3.q19! This attacks the four Black men, and after they are defended with 4.s16, capturing r16, they are again attacked with 5.r18, forcing Black to fill at r16. Then t18 leaves four points in the corner in White's hands, while Black has nothing to show but one prisoner. Had he prevented White's invasion in the manner indicated above, he would have had eleven points in the corner in addition to the prisoner, and White's territory would have been reduced by the three points p19, o19, o18. Thus, White has gained fully eighteen points by the invasion.

In the lower right corner we have almost a mirror picture of the position in the left corner. However, there is an all important difference. After 1.q2, p2; 3.s2, q1; 5.r2, Black's man on p2 requires no protection against capture as did the man on d2. Black could therefore proceed with 6.s4, depriving White of the space he needs to make two eyes. The only chance for White to live in the corner would lie in producing a Ko by

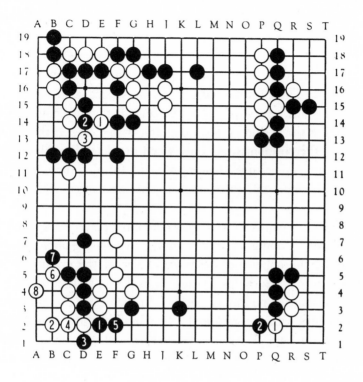

ABCDEFGHIJKLMNOPQRST

DIAGRAM 11

playing 5.r1 instead of r2. The continuation would then be
6.r2*;[1] 7.s5, s6; 9.q2*, and if White has more Ko threats than
Black, the latter must finally play p1, whereupon White has
time to form Me by placing men on s4 and s1.

An important thing to know is the minimum number of
vacant points which a group must enclose in order to be safe

---

[1] A * indicates the capture of one stone. A figure following a * indicates the
number of stones taken, if more than one is captured.

against any attack. This number depends upon whether it is the move of the defending or the attacking player. If the defending player moves, only three adjacent vacant points are needed to form two Me, while even four are sometimes insufficient if the attacking player has the move. All possible arrangements of four vacant adjacent points are shown in Diagram 12. These formations can, of course, occur in the middle of the board just as well as on the edge. If the four points form a square, the position is lost no matter who moves. If they form a Tee, the position is safe only when the defending player has the move and occupies the central point, forming three Me. The other three possible formations are safe no matter whose move it is.

If the two points on which the defending player has his choice to place the saving stone forming the two Me are already occupied by the opponent, as shown in one of the examples, the position is evidently lost because then the separation of the adjacent points is no longer possible. In such cases the minimum number of vacancies required is five. It will be seen that as soon as the attacking player attempts to surround completely a chain containing five points, he fails, because when there is only one point left, the defending player captures the four opposing stones within his group, thus creating four adjacent vacancies which save him.

Out of twelve possible arrangements of five adjacent vacant points the two shown in Diagram 12 are not safe when the attacking player moves, as can easily be verified.

Thirty-five different arrangements of six adjacent vacant points are possible, but they are all safe except the one shown in Diagram 6.

Chains containing seven or more adjacent vacant points are safe against all attacks, though there is one position containing

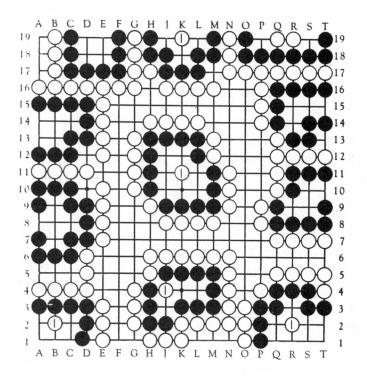

DIAGRAM 12

seven points which the attacking player can enter without losing his men because a Seki results. This position is also shown in Diagram 12. White plays 1.k11, 2.i11; 3.k12, 4.k10; 5.l11, and neither player can occupy l10 or i12.

Seki can also very often be reached by the attacking player when the vacant points in the defending chain comprise a corner and the two points adjoining the corner, and in these cases the statements made about chains comprising four or more adjacent vacant points do not apply. In the position shown in the lower left corner, for instance, White wins by 1. b2, threatening to continue with a2 and c2. The Black group would then be attacked, since c1 would be the only point left which is directly adjacent to it. 2.b1 would not save Black, because after 3.a2 he cannot make two eyes with c2 on account of 4.c1, which would again capture all Black men. 2.a2 would be of no avail either, because White would occupy b1 and then any two of the remaining three vacant points, with the result that upon capturing the four intruders Black remains with a position containing four points in the losing position illustrated previously.

In the lower right-hand corner White would reach either Seki or Ko by playing 1.r2, depending upon how Black continues: 2.s2; 3.s1, 4.t2 would result in a Seki, while 4.t1 might lead to Ko by way of 5.r1, 6.q1; 7.t2.*

The assumption in all cases illustrated in Diagram 12 has been that the attacking player cannot threaten to separate part of the surrounded group as in the position shown in the lower centre. Here White would win with 1.i4, because he attacks four men which can be defended only by 2.i3, whereupon 3.k4 prevents the formation of two Me.

Building impregnable positions

Let us now examine a few examples illustrated in Diagram 13 which show how, in an actual game, groups are formed in a corner which are able to develop two eyes against any attack the opponent might institute.

In the lower left corner we will assume the following introductory sequence of moves: 1.f3, c7; 3.c3, d3; 5.c4, d5; 7.b5,

[38]

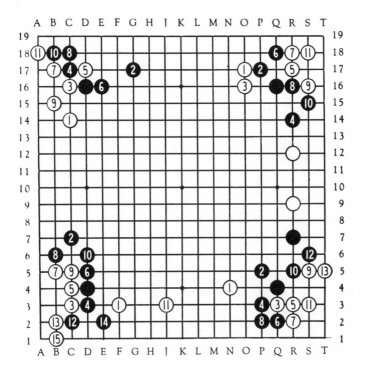

DIAGRAM 13

b6; 9.c5, d6; 11. i3. The reason for this move will be explained in a later chapter. It has nothing to do with the fight in the corner which we want to discuss here.

Black now proceeds to attack the white chain by playing 12.c2, but cannot capture it against correct defence. The best way for White to gain space for Me is evidently 13.b2, forcing Black to protect himself against the threat d2 by either d2, d1, or e2, and 15.b1. This just barely saves the White group, for after 16.a5; 17.a4, a6, 19. b3, White has two Me.

If in the position shown in the diagram Black's man were located on c6 instead of c7, White, on the move, would have to add a stone at b3, reaching one of the fundamental positions given in Diagram 12. Black on the move, however, would win the group by 16.a4; 17.a5, b3, as 19. b4 would lead to immediate capture through 20.a6.

In other words, if the stone c7 had been placed on c6, White would not have had time for 11. i3, but he would have had to expand immediately with 11. a6, a7; 13. a5, b7 (necessary to protect a7); 15. d2, e2; 17. c2, e3; 19.e1, f1; 21.d1,f2; 23. b2. Without the last move Black would still have had a chance to attack White and to produce a Seki or Ko similarly to the way shown in conjunction with the position in the lower right corner of Diagram 12.

The position in the upper left of the Diagram shows a version of the same opening, with the difference that here White advances on his third move only as far as c16 instead of c17. After 4.c17, d17, Black's simplest continuation is 6.e16, permitting a more or less equal division of the territory by 7.b17, c18; 9.b15, b18; 11.a18.

White could secure more territory by playing 9.b18 instead of b15. But after 10.d18, c15 Black would have Sente, while, in the line illustrated in the Diagram, Sente is retained by White. He threatens d18, winning Black's three men in the corner, so that Black must make one more move to ward off this threat and White can take the initiative on another part of the board, or he can further increase his territory on the upper left by an extension downward, probably as far as d10.

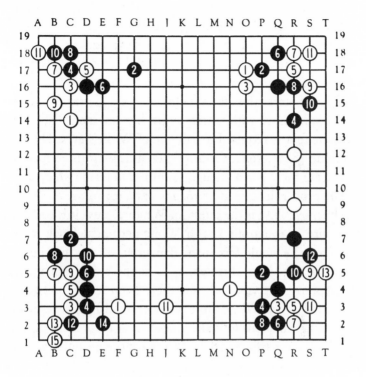

DIAGRAM 13

In the symmetrical position reached after White's move 5.d17, any extension of the stones clustered in the corner is desirable, rather than a move attacking one of these stones directly. Instead of 6.e16, Black might play 6.c18, for example, whereupon White would extend with b16. 8.d15 White could counter with 9.d18. Black must spend three moves to kill the intruders, giving White time to secure part of the corner without losing Sente: 10.e17, b18; 12.e18, b17; 14.d19.

The position in the lower right corner came about as follows: 1.n4,p5; 3.q3,p3; 5.r3,q2; 7.r2,p2; 9.s5,r5; 11.s3,s6; 13.t5. The White group is now safe against attack because one eye will be created in the space s4–t4 and another in the space t1–t2.

If Black starts the attack with 14.r1, 15. s1, t2, White must not waste a move with taking on q1, because then Black would gain the tempo required to kill one of White's eyes. He would continue 18. s4; 19.r4, t6; 21.t4*, t3, attacking three men, and after 23.s4 there is not enough room left to form two eyes.

The proper defence after 16.t2 is 17.t3, t6; 19. s4.

The move 11.s3 is the safest for White because it is best suited to ensure an eye around s2. If White permitted Black to occupy s2 or t2 he would face many dangerous threats. For instance: 11. r4, s6; 13.t4, s2, threatening to connect with r1; 15.r1, s3, threatening s4, 17.s4; and now there is no room for two eyes. Instead of 15. r1, White must play s1. This barely saves his life, because he threatens to make an eye on t1 by playing t2, and if Black prevents this by 16. t2 White continues with 17. s3 and thus secures two eyes.

After 14. t2 (instead of s2), 15. r1, 16.t3; 17.s3 would lose, because after 18.t6 White cannot play t5 since Black would capture three men on s4. He must therefore let Black occupy t5, and the eye on s4 is thus destroyed. Neither is 15.t3, t6; 17.t5 playable on account of 18. s3, which attacks four men and wins the whole group after 19.s4, s2. Only 17. s2 will save White, because after 18.s4, t1* either r1 or t5 will make another eye. He saves his life also after 14. t6, by playing 15. t2,s3; 17.s2; or, if 16. t5, 17.s4,s1; 19.r1, s2; 21.s3. Not so good would be 15.r1, because after t5, 17.s4, t2; 19. s2, t3, the life of White's group will depend upon the outcome of a Ko on t1 and s1.

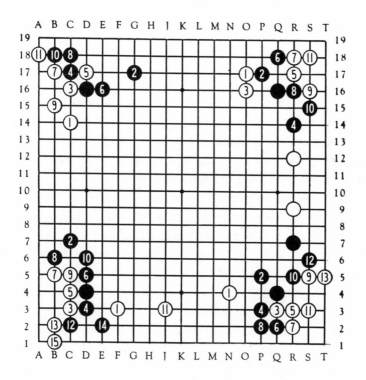

DIAGRAM 13

The position in the upper right corner shows how a very small space may be sufficient to build two eyes in if the surrounding group of the adversary is connected only loosely so that a counter-attack is possible.

After 1.o17, p17; 3.o16, r14, White can play r17 and obtain a living group in the corner as follows: 5.r17, q18; 7. r18, r16; 9, s16, s15; 11. s18. This threatens t17, which would ensure one eye on s17 and another t19. Black cannot prevent this by 12.t16, because White would play 13.q17 with the threat p18, and Black cannot save his man on q18 with 14.o18 on account of 15.p.16, p18; 17.n18, leaving only three vacant points for Black's four men, while White's group has still four breathing-spaces. The finishing moves might be: 18.n19; 19.m18 (not m19, because 20.m18 21.o19*, n17; 23.n19, 1 19, would kill the white men), 20.r19; 21.s19; and all Black has is a Ko with very slim chances for profit, because after 22.p19; 23.q19* White has still four breathing-spaces, and Black has only one.

Sometimes apparently lost armies are saved by very much more subtle manœuvres than those illustrated in Diagram 13. In the position shown in the lower left of Diagram 14 the four White men seem past hope, as the connection between the Blacks on c1 and f2 cannot be prevented and there is not enough space on lines a and b to form two Me.

If White had a man on b1, he could secure two eyes by playing b4 and then either a2 or a3. But if White, who is on the move, starts out with b1 Black replies b4 and White can make only one eye, either around a1 or around c1. For if White captures c1 by playing d1, Black puts a man on a2 and answers a3 with b3, whereupon the eye on a1 is false. And if, instead of playing d1, White first forms an eye by a2, Black connects his man c1 by playing d1.

The proper course of play for White is suggested by the idea that if it were possible to make the move b1 with a second threat, in addition to the threat b4, Black would not have time to destroy the second Me by playing b4.

This second threat is prepared by 1.e2, e1; 3.d1, d2*. Now the move 5.b1 threatens c2, which either would produce two eyes by the capture of two men on d1, or, if Black fills in on d1,

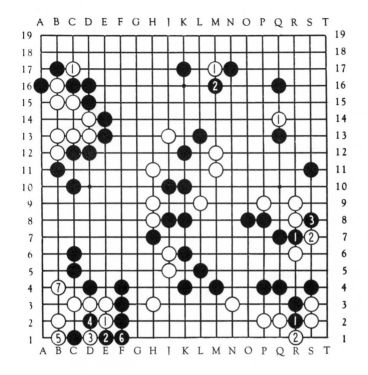

DIAGRAM 14

would capture four men on f1 with the threat either to make an escape for the White army with g2 or to form two eyes by playing d1.

Therefore Black has not time to play 6.b4, but must first save his men by 6.f1. Then White continues with 7.b4, and all attempts of Black to hinder the formation of two Me must fail.

For instance: 8. a3; 9.a2, a4; 11. b5, etc. Not 11. a5, on account of b5; 13.c2*, a4; 15.a6, b7; 17.a7, a8; 19.a3*, b6; 21.b8; and White has only one eye.

White could interchange the order of the third and fifth moves, because if Black, after 3.b1, tried to stop White with b4, White would play 5.d1 and obtain his two eyes in the same way as shown in the main variation.

However, a transposition of the first and fifth moves would not work; for after 1.b1,b4; 3.e2 Black would reply not, e1, but d1, and if White prevents the connection on e1, Black continues with 6.a2, destroying the eye in the corner as shown before.

The position in the upper left of the diagram shows an even more surprising example of the rescue of an apparently lost group by an attack on a weak link in the surrounding chain which gains the tempo for the move required to secure two Me.

If White started out with a15, Black would reduce White's erritory with a12 to less than the minimum needed for two eyes. Taking Black's man a16 with a17 would, of course, produce only a false eye, because the stone a17 can be attacked sooner or later.

Again, 1.a12 would not secure Me, because of 2.a14; 3.a15, b14; or 3.b14, a15; 5.a13,a17; 7. c17, c18; and the White man is lost through Sh'cho.

The ingenious method by which White saves his group is this: He first plays c17. Black has two ways of capturing this man, beginning either with c18 or with d17.

Let us first consider the play after 2.c18. White continues with 3.d17, e17; 5.d18, e18; 7.b18. This is a double attack and Black must therefore capture the three White men with 8.d19. Now White plays 9.a18, threatening a17, which would not only attack b17 but also prepare the formation of a second eye with

[46]

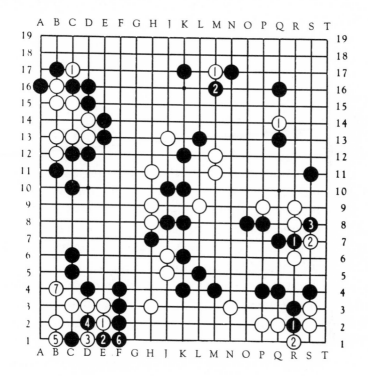

DIAGRAM 14

b19, the three White men in the corner connecting with the main army through the capture of the Black man at a16.

Black must therefore prevent this combination by playing 10.b19. However, White is now safe because he can follow one of the lines originally sketched: 11.a12, a14; 13.b14; and Black cannot connect with a15 because 15.a13 would win three men,

[47]

since a17 cannot be played on account of 17.c17, capturing five men.

It would not have been good for White to play 3.b18 instead of giving up three men first, because Black might have answered a18, throwing the position into Ko.

If Black, in answer to White's first move, replies d17, a very similar combination results. White would continue 3.c18, b18; 5.b19, d18; and now again 7. a12, a14; 9.b14; and Black cannot connect with a15 because after 11.a13 three men are lost, as a17 would be answered by a18, capturing six men.

In the first variation discussed above, the argument might be made that Black, after 1.c17,c18; 3.d17, could form a safe group in the corner with 4.a18, thus ensuring the capture of the White army. However, White can develop his two men on c17 and d17 into a group which survives just long enough to kill the Black men in the corner. For after 5.e17 Black has not time to play b19, because of the threat e15, which would win three men and free the White army. Black must first play 6.f16, and now White prevents the formation of two Me by 7.b19, d18; 9. e18, f17; 11.b18, etc.

In answer to 9.b18 instead of first e18 Black would still have the chance to throw the position into Ko with c19.

In an actual game good players always try to avoid situations in which an army is so closely beset by the enemy that it can barely escape capture by making just two eyes. As a rule they are satisfied with the ability to form one secure eye within a group which is sandwiched between hostile forces and they try to connect that group safely with another one which contains at least one eye. Such connections are commonly effected somewhere in the middle of the board, all armies the bases of which are formed near the edge trying to develop toward the centre.

[48]

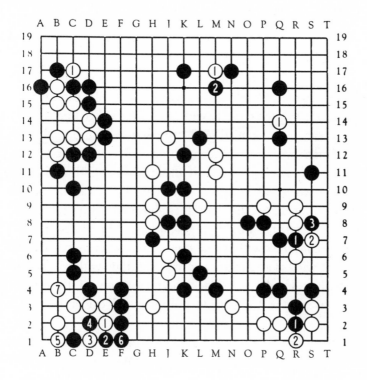

DIAGRAM 14

For reasons similar to those just discussed, stones intended to expand the territory of a group should be placed so that the adversary cannot prevent their connection. While directly adjacent placement of two men in a straight line is the only con-

Maintaining lines of communication

[49]

nection which can neither be broken nor even threatened, such safe connections are usually materialized only in the course of **hand to hand fights. Ordinarily the stones are strung farther** apart in order to make possible their use for the walling off of as much territory as feasible.

Two stones in a straight line, separated by one vacant point, are safely connected only in the second line. If Black in Diagram 14 plays r2, White connects with r1. In any other line the connection can be broken, though this is usually profitable only if the man breaking the connection can communicate with others in the neighbourhood. If Black plays r7 and White connects the two separated groups with s7, Black can break that connection again because he can establish communication with either s4 or s11. He would play s6, and if White kills this man by s5, he continues with s8 and then connects via s9. Black could also start with s8 and in answer to s9 continue with s6 and connect with s5. However, if Black had no man on s11, the connection between the two White groups could evidently not be broken.

On the third line of the board two men are usually safely connected even with two vacant points intervening, again provided the attacking player has no other troops in the neighbourhood with which the men attempting the break might communicate.

If White, in Diagram 14, plays m17 Black wins this man with m16, threatening m18 with Sh'cho, for if White tries to defend with 3.m18, Black replies n18 and the two men cannot escape.

On the fourth line two intervening vacant spaces usually enable the opponent to separate two men. White's man q14 cannot be captured by 2.p14. White could extend with 3.r15, for instance, and the continuation might be: r14; 5.q15, p15; 7. r13, s14; 9.s15, s13 (to save the two men which had only two

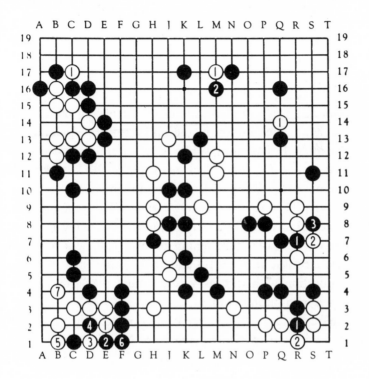

DIAGRAM 14

breathing-spaces left); 11.r16,q17; 13.r17, r18; 15.s18, q18; 17.s19, and White has enough room to make two Me.

In the middle of the board the safest connection is the form shown on i8,k8,i10,k10, which evidently cannot be intercepted. Also k12 is safely connected because k11 would be answered with i11, and after White protects his man, Black continues with i12. The diagonal connection, as in k12–l13, or in k4–l5

[51]

k6, is also safe, because as soon as the aggressor occupies one of the two vacant adjacent squares the defending player plays on the other.

If White breaks the connection between k6 and k8 with k7, Black can re-establish it by l7, followed by l8, or he can connect with h7 by attacking on i7 instead of l7.

It is surprising over what a long distance a connection can sometimes be established in spite of the menacing presence of hostile men. The position in the upper right of Diagram 15 is an example. It looks as if White were certain of a good sized territory around the lone Black man, for if Black makes the obvious move o17 White replies n17 and then n18.

However, Black can force a connection of his men, and with it a reduction of the White territory, in the following manner: He starts with 1.o18, threatening to play n18, which would safely connect the man on l18 and at the same time maintain communication with q17, as White cannot play p18 without losing two men through o17.

White replies 2. n18, and after Black threatens the capture of this man with 3. n17 White plays 4.o17. Now it would not do for Black to proceed with m18, because White would continue with p18 and the Black group would be lost, for White would destroy with m17 the eye which the Black group has on n18 after the capture of n17.

Instead, Black connects with 5.p18, and after White's m17 he continues with 7.n19. If White takes Black's man, m18 establishes the desired connection, and if he plays m18 himself, Black replies m19, and again l18 is connected.

The position in the upper left of the diagram shows a Black group on line h which appears lost, as it is sandwiched between White groups and does not comprise enough territory within its reach to form two Me. However, some of the men of the surrounding White groups are not as safely connected as shown

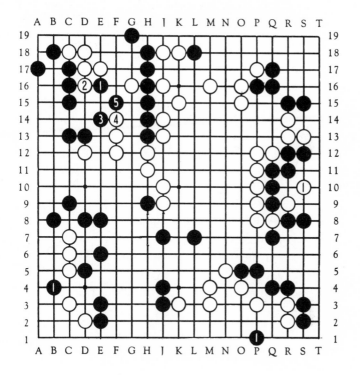

DIAGRAM 15

in the examples of Diagram 14, and their loose contour gives Black the opportunity to break through, connecting himself with the group on line c.

The weakest link in White's chain is e14. But if Black plays there to start with, White can maintain his line of communication because after f14, 3.f15 he catches this man with g15.

This suggests as the best plan to start with 1.e16, because now the moves e14 and f15 would attack the man on e15 so that White would not have time to play g15 and Black could occupy this spot, completing the break. For instance: 1.e16, d16; 3.e14, f14; 5.f15, f16; 7. g15. The White army on lines 15 to 18 is now cut off, and it is lost because there is not enough space for two Me. For instance 8.f18; 9.g17, f17; 11.d15, c19; 13.e19. White has only one eye.

White might try f16 in answer to Black's first move. This would, indeed, maintain his line of communication if Black would again continue with e14, because now 4. f14 would make f15 inaccessible.

But Black would play 3.f14, e14; 5.d16, with the threat to cut off four White men with f17 and in this way to connect the two Black armies. White has not time to prevent this cut with 6.g17, because 7.f15 would again cut off the White group, this time taking in seven men. There is not room for Me because after 8.f18 Black plays 9.g18, e19; 11.c19.

In the position in the lower right corner of Diagram 15 Black can steal a good part of White's territory with 1.p1, which threatens both the cut at q3 and the connection at r1. White cannot defend these two threats with 2.q2, because of the loose diagonal connection of his men at p3 and o4 which permits this neat combination: 3.r1, q1; 5.p2! Now four White men are attacked and they cannot be saved by capturing the stone on r1, for Black would isolate them by cutting at q3. Neither can White escape by playing 6.q3 himself, since 7.o3 would then attack six of his men and he could neither defend them with p4, which would leave his chain only one liberty at n5, nor capture at s1 as Black would then catch his men by occuping p4. The best reply to Black's first move would be 2.p2, r1; 4.o1, q1; 6.o2.

White, on the move in the position along the right edge,

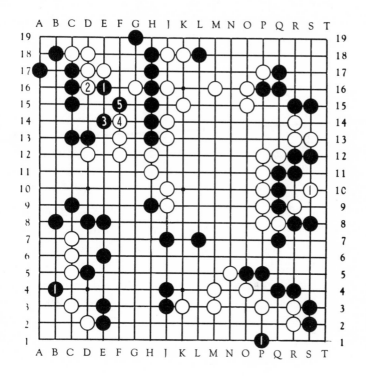

DIAGRAM 15

could ruin Black's territory between lines 8 and 12 with 1.s10. This invader would safely connect with the stone on s13. In reply to 2.t12 White would play 3.t11, and if Black then attacked r9 with s9 or r10, White would defend his man and Black could not approach upon s11 because his group would have only one liberty left and die. Neither could Black save himself with 4.s11. White would reply 5.t10, and after s9; 7.t13,r10* he would capture Black's men with 9.r9. Thus, Black must be satisfied to answer 1.s10 with s9, permitting 3.t11,r10*; 5.t12.

Had it been Black's first move, he could have stopped White with 1.t13,t14; 3.t12, when s10 would have failed against s9, etc. Here Sente was, therefore, worth nine points to White.

Throwing a position into Ko In the lower left of Diagram 15 Black's invasion at b4 would destroy White's group unless it can save itself in a Ko fight. Play might proceed as follows: 1.b4,c4; 3.b2,c2 (necessary to prevent Black from occupying this point and connecting via d3 or d1); 5.a5,b3; 7.a7,a2; 9.b1 (otherwise White gets two Me), a4, and after 11.b5,a6; 13.b6*, b7 Black cannot fill at a6 as White would capture his six men with a8, so that he must play 15.a3*, whereupon the outcome of this Ko will decide the battle.

Had Black taken a4 right away on his eleventh move, the continuaation b5; 13.a1*,a4*; 15.a6, would have let White form two eyes with c1; 17.b4*,a2*[3]; 19.a4,b1. White would lose his group, however, if he answered 15.a6 with b4, as the sacrifice of five men through 17.a2 would not leave White room for two eyes.

The chances of saving a surrounded army by throwing it into Ko are usually best when the attacking group itself is subject to a good many Ko threats. The upper right of Diagram 16 illustrates such a case.

Black would start with 1.s15, and White would prevent the formation of an eye around r15 with 2.q15, at the same time preparing to play r15 in reply to 3.t14, and thus turning s14 into a false eye. After Black continues with 3.s18, threatening to secure two Me with s19, White will play s19 himself. Then 5.t16 will make sure of one eye as s17 could be answered

[56]

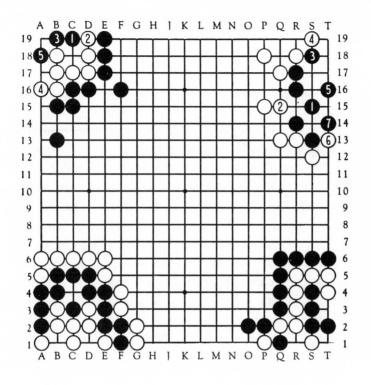

DIAGRAM 16

by t18, and a second eye would be created with men on s14 and t14 if White did not now play 6.t13. After 7.t14 and 18.s14* Black's eye on t15 will be genuine only if he can fill the Ko at s14. He has excellent prospects of winning the Ko because he has a considerable number of threats to break through the surrounding chain of White men: q19, to start with, followed by either q18 or r19; then q14 and q16, and also t18, threatening s17.

An important configuration to study is the position in the upper left corner, as it frequently arises in actual play. Black can prevent the formation of Me with 1.c19,d19; 3.b19,a16; 5.a18. The result is a Seki if White leaves the intruders alone. He can capture them only if he has more compelling Ko threats than Black so that he can risk throwing the position into Ko with 6.a17. If Black had the same number of valid threats he would win through a neat sacrifice: 7.a19,c18*[4]; 9.b19. This would threaten to prevent the formation of Me by a19. Therefore White would have to play there himself, and now the Ko is produced in such a way that Black makes the first capture and White must make the first Ko threat. After White runs out of his threats, Black plays a19, sacrificing three men, and then he occupies a19 again, leaving insufficient room for White to live. With the last Ko threat available to White, however, he would in the end be able to capture the man on b19, forming two Me.

It would have been a fatal mistake for White to attack the Black intruders with 6.c18 instead of a17. Black would have replied 7.a15, and after 8.a19*[2] he could have recaptured, preventing White from approaching further. This situation would not result in a Seki but in a loss for White, for as soon as no more Ko threats are on the board, Black could play a19 and c19, sacrificing four men as shown above and then destroying White's eyes with b19, etc. This illustrates the only exception where four liberties in the shape on an L do not guaranty enough room for two Me.

There are two more unique cases, rarely seen in actual play.

Positions are thinkable in which three or more Kos are open at the same time, so that a game would have to be called a draw

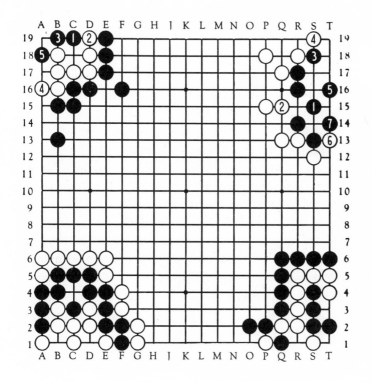

DIAGRAM 16

if the players persist in keeping the Kos open and in taking and retaking the men in them alternately.

The position in the lower left corner of Diagram 16 shows such a case. White threatens to capture the whole Black chain with c4. Black, on the move, plays 1.b1, threatening in his turn to take all White men with d1. White replies c4, and Black plays d1. Now White retakes in the first Ko on a1, Black second on c3, White in the third on e1, etc.

If White on the rest on the board has an advantage of more than eighteen points, he will permit Black to capture his group in this corner, because this would mean just eighteen points to Black, so that he would still lose the game, while a draw would result if the moves were repeated indefinitely.

To give up the fight for his fourteen men would mean 29 points less for Black, and he would do so willingly if he is more than 29 points ahead in the rest of the game.

Another possible draw by repetition of moves is shown in the lower right corner of the diagram. White, on the move, attacks four Black men with 1.t1. Black can take two men with r1, but White recaptures two men with 3.s1, and if Black plays q1 the position of the diagram is reached again.

If Black has an advantage of more than eight points in the game, he will give up his four men rather than repeat the moves, and White will reason the same way if he has an advantage of more than twenty points. If White permits Black to move, he will play 1.t3 and win the White chain, as after t1, which captures five men, Black will reply 3.s3, whereupon the White group has only one eye.

The only other case in which a draw is thinkable is one in which both players have the same number of points at the end of the game. This does happen once in a while, but, of course, very rarely.

The proper way to start a game

The study of the examples presented up to this point will serve the beginner as a good preparation for the hand to hand fights with which every game of Go is replete. But a reasonably intelligent conduct of the opening, where such fights occur only rarely, requires at least a cursory acquaintance with some of the elementary positional principles that guide the choice of the initial moves. Most frequently the intersection of the third and fourth lines is chosen for the first move, that is r4 or p3, or any of the corresponding points in the other corners. In

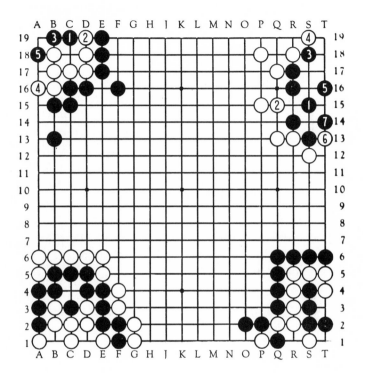

DIAGRAM 16

conjunction with r4 a man on either q3 or p3 would almost surely secure the corner, for the invading enemy could not find room enough to make two eyes in.

A player of attacking temperament will probably answer 1.r4 with 2.p3 in order to make it a little more difficult for Black to secure the corner. But instead of making a move of such attacking character a more peaceful reply would be just as good, such as d3 or r16, which prepares to secure another corner.

After gaining a foothold in one or two of the corners, the players usually extend their corner positions along the edge of the board, with stones placed close enough to make it dangerous for the opponent to invade the territory thus outlined. Instead of such peaceful positional play, an attacking type of player will probably again prefer to approach more closely the corners in which the opponent has started to fortify himself.

It is naturally the desire of the players to stake off as large territories as possible; but they are restrained in forming plans too ambitious by the ever present danger of the opponent separating their outposts by an invasion into the territory they were preparing to secure.

Whenever possible, a player combines attack and defence in the same move. That is, he tries to make such moves as will not only consolidate the territory he has previously staked off, but will also threaten to invade territory sketched by the opponent.

A move involving a threat which the opponent must answer in order not to be put at a disadvantage is said to be made with "Sente." To gain and maintain Sente is very desirable because the opponent is kept busy and cannot easily assume the initiative himself. Of course, it is not possible to keep Sente throughout the game. Usually Sente changes rather frequently from one player to the other, because it will often happen that a player considers a certain threat of the opponent less important than an attack he can make himself.

During the opening stage of the game Sente expresses itself only through threats to wall off large territories. In the middle game Sente usually involves threats against one or more men in hand to hand fights or threats to cut through lines of communication, or threats to hinder the formation of two Me in a group which is surrounded. Such threats should never be made unless they consolidate territory at the same time, thus resulting in a definite advantage. Moves which merely threaten something the opponent can defend, without at the same time securing additional territory, should be left for Ko situations, in which that player always gains an advantage who. has more threats at his disposal.

All beginners make the mistake to start hand to hand fights too early. Usually they try to attack every stone which the opponent places, instead of pausing to stake off territory, which must obviously be the better plan since there are more vacant points available for capture than hostile men.

During the many centuries of Go history a goodly number of capable analysts have devoted painstaking efforts to the problems involved in the conduct of the opening, and many books have been published by Go masters on the subject of "Joseki," or opening play in a corner. For many generations the contents of these books were memorized by ardent students of the game, with the same negative results with which Chess-lovers memorize variations of Chess openings. Proficiency at Chess or Go or any other game of mental skill is never attained by memorizing a great number of possible variations, but by understanding the general principles which govern good play in any position.

I shall therefore confine myself to listing some of the frequently recurring opening moves in a table as a matter of record, and I shall try to evolve general guiding principles of opening play according to which a player can find his way in any opening without the necessity of burdening his memory.

The detailed development of these general principles will be taken up in the third chapter of this book. For the moment we will merely discuss a few elementary considerations which will help the understanding of problems of the sort which arise after

[63]

the first few moves in the corners of the board.

Let us assume that, as suggested above, Black has started the game with 1.r4 and White has replied 2.p3. If Black wants to secure the corner right away he can do so by playing either 3.q2 or 3.q3. In answer to q2 there would be no sense in White's advancing against the corner with 4.q3, because Black would stop him with 5.r3, thus securing about ten points in the corner while White has not as yet walled off any territory to speak of. White would make matters worse by continuing his attack— if his play may be so termed—with 6.p2, which threatens to win the man on q2 with r2. Instead of protecting this man, Black would place a man near one of the three other corners, threatening to secure large territory while White's 8.r2; 9.s2, 10.q1* yields only about six points, made up of one prisoner, one point of territory gained, and a reduction of Black's territory in the corner by four points.

A further great advantage gained by Black in this transaction is the fact that he has retained Sente. There is no immediate threat against the three Black men in the corner available to White, and so Black can follow up his seventh move, which might have been at q17, with 9.r15 or r14 securing about twelve points in the corner.

From these considerations it is evident that White, instead of 4.q3, should have played m3 or any other move sketching out an amount of territory approximately equal to that walled off by Black in the corner.

If Black had played 3.q3, White's best answer would have been p4. At first sight it looks as if Black had much the better of this position, as he has secured about nine points in the corner, while White has only prepared to secure an equivalent, with l3 for example, so that Black could spoil White's plan by placing a man on l3 himself. However, White's fourth move

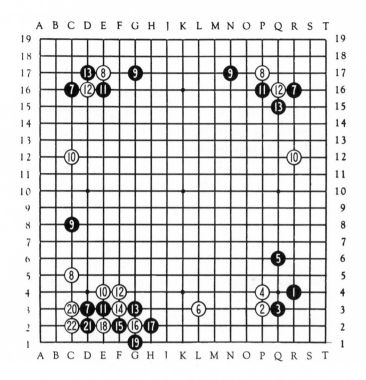

DIAGRAM 17

does involve a slight threat against the corner, arising from the fact that the two White men are solidly connected while Black's two men can still be threatened with separation.

In answer to Black's 5.m3 White might play 6.q4, threatening to cut at r3, and after Black has connected with 7.r3, White might continue with 8.r5, confining Black's group in the cor-

[65]

ner, in fact menacing its life. For if Black permits 10.s4; 11.s3, s5, it is very dubious whether he has enough space left to form Me. He will therefore have to defend himself with either 9.s4, s5; 11.s2, or with 9.s5, s6; 11.t4, q6; 13.s2, and in both cases White has retained Sente, which he can utilize to stake off considerable territory with r9 or even r10. This long jump would be justified in view of the fact that White has developed a strong wall all around the Black position in the corner, so that he needs to strengthen only the other side of the territory staked off, in case Black threatens to invade it later.

In view of these possibilities it seems best for Black to heed the threat involved in White's fourth move p4 by playing 5.q6 or s6 or s7, which would prevent White from enclosing the corner from the top. White can then continue with 6. l 3, and Black can now play elsewhere with Sente.

As long as the other corners are not yet approached, he will use Sente to gain a foothold in any one of them. If such preliminary foothold has already been established, he will make a move somewhere near one of the edges, probably on the third line, midway between two corners, with the intention of establishing connection with one of the two corner outposts, depending upon where the opponent replies.

No matter where a player places a man during the opening stage of the game, he must never lose sight of the two responsibilities which this stone has: one of connecting with other men placed near the edge so that at least one eye can be formed by them in case of attack by the adversary, and the other of maintaining communication with the centre of the board, to connect there with other men who in their turn are seeking friendly groups because they themselves belong to a chain which has only one eye near the corner or the edge. Even if a group has enough space near the edge to form two Me, its development into the

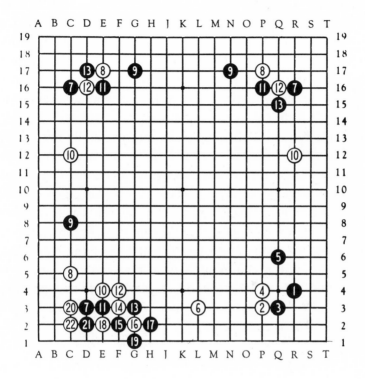

DIAGRAM 17

centre of the board is important, quite apart from the fact that there it may serve as a haven of refuge for less fortunate friendly groups. For it might otherwise easily happen that the opponent, by walling off the entrances to the centre, gains considerable territory in the middle of the board. Such an example is shown in the game analysed at the end of this chapter.

[67]

Now let us assume that Black, on his seventh move, plays d3, and White answers c5, and Black this time immediately sandwiches White's man by 9.c8. The beginner will be tempted to go closer, playing c7 or even c6. But it is well to consider that as strongly as we press upon an opposing man, that man presses back on us, unless our man is more closely connected to a friendly group. We will show this later by another example in the upper right corner of Diagram 17.

White can either develop his man c5 peacefully toward the middle of the board with 10.e5 or f5, or he can, more aggressively, continue e4; 11.e3, f4; 13.g3, f3; 15.f2, g2. This threatens to capture g3 with h3, as Black cannot play g4 on account of g5, etc., which would lead to a Sh'cho. Black will therefore take White's man with 17.h2, thus incidentally providing an escape of his chain d3–h2 into the middle of the board (g4; 19.h3, h4; 21.i4), and White will in turn establish himself in the corner: e2; 19.g1*, c3; 21.d2, c2. Black would now probably develop his man on c8 by c11, and White would take Sente at one of the remaining corners.

The fact that White has sacrificed two men (on the sixteenth and eighteenth moves) has not meant a loss. The advantage gained through this sacrifice in the corner outweighs the sacrifice a good deal.

The position in the upper right of Diagram 17 shows the development which might take place if after the same original formation which we observed in the other corners Black approaches White more closely.

We will assume that after the play in the lower right corner Black has used Sente to occupy r16, White has answered p17, and Black plays 9.n17. This move is probably not very good, because White, after strengthening his man with p16, is near enough to both Black men to exert a threat on them. If Black

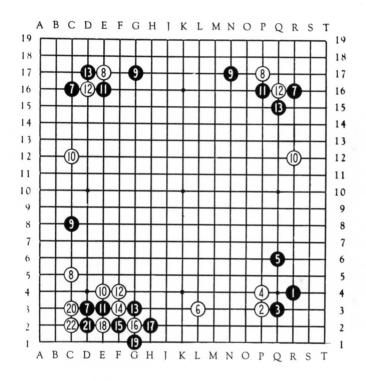

DIAGRAM 17

replies 11.r13, White will first attack n17 with n16 and after 13.m17 will extend into the corner with r17; 15.s17, r18. White has thus a safe group, which has access to the centre. He could also have played 10.r12, permitting Black to attack with 11.p16, as shown in the diagram. After q16; 13.q15, q17; 15. o16, r17; 17.s15, s16; 19.r15, r9, White has a safe group on line r and also in the corner. 21.s17, s18; 23.t16*, would mean very little for Black, as White can ensure Me with t18.

To cut the connection between the two men which White has placed on the eighth and twelfth moves would not be good, because Black's men could not all be connected safely afterwards without the loss of Sente. The position in the upper left corner illustrates the play which might ensue: 7.c16, e17; 9.g17, c12; 11.e16, d16; 13.d17, d15. If it were not for the fact that Black has a man on q6, White could now win the man on e16 with f16 through Sh'cho. As it is, Black has time to play 15. c17, but after 16.c15 Black will have to make one more move to connect his men, such as e18; otherwise White would still have many threats left against the corner as well as against the side by developing his man on e17 with f16 followed by f17.

End game play When the game has reached the phase in which the opposing armies are in more or less close contact everywhere, delineating the territories they have conquered, there are always a few more points to be gained by the player on the move where the frontier lines have not yet reached the edges of the board. In some of these endings Sente is retained, in others it is lost. To select the proper order in which to play the endings it is necessary to count the number of points at stake in each of them.

Diagram 18 shows the position arrived at after 136 moves in the game given at the end of this chapter. It is clear that all corners except the lower left are in Black's hands, and White controls the large vacant space in the centre in addition to the lower left corner. It is also clear that the White group on the lower edge between lines i and q is lost and that the Black men in the right centre between the 9th and 12th lines cannot evade capture.

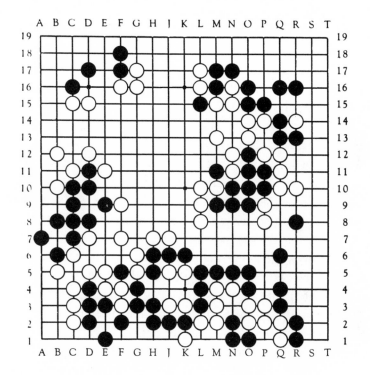

A B C D E F G H J K L M N O P Q R S T

DIAGRAM 18

It is Black's move. Let us examine step by step how many points can be gained at different parts of the board by the player who starts.

In the upper left corner Black could extend his frontier as far as i19, and after i18; 3.h19, k18; 5.g18, h18, the White territory is four or five points smaller than it would have been had it been

White's move in this position so that he could have played g18. Black would not continue with 7.k19, because after 1 19 he would have to fill in at g19, and Sente would go over to White.

On the left edge Black could play b15, and this would make a difference of six points as against the position which would result if White started with b 16. But whoever makes the advance at this point loses Sente. After 1.b15, b14; 3.a15, a14, Black must guard against b16, and if White starts, he must protect himself similarly after b16; b17, a16; a17.

The same difference of six points with loss of Sente is at stake on the upper right at l 18 and m18.

At the right edge it would make a difference of about six or seven or eight points for whoever occupies s9 first. If Black plays 1.s9, s10; 3.t10, t11; 5.t9, s11, the points s8 and t8 are included in his territory while above the eighth line the vacant points are all filled in as far as the eleventh line. If White starts with s9 and continues with t8, Black's territory is filled in as far down as the seventh line, while s10, s11, t10, and t11 remain open for White. This means a difference of six points, and the player who starts retains Sente.

Only about three or four points are at stake between the eleventh and thirteenth lines on the right edge, and the player who starts retains Sente, as a few tries will show.

In the lower left corner only one point is to be gained at a5, and two at c1.

Three points can be gained by Black through playing m7, n7, and o7, because each of these moves threatens to save the nine men which White has almost completely surrounded. Then there are one or two points to be gained by playing e10, as this threatens not only to continue f10 but also to cut at e12 with an attack on e11, thus gaining time for d13 and c13, which would greatly endanger the White group on the upper left.

[72]

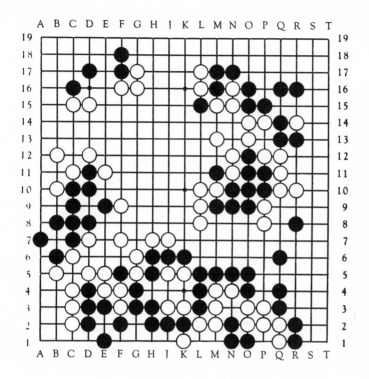

DIAGRAM 18

Finally, there are about three or four points at stake at e7, one point at k7, and about three points at p7.

Black has much the better chance to make most of the contestable points because in the majority of the cases mentioned Sente is retained by the player who starts.

The game actually ended as follows:

137.	e	7	e	6
139.	d	6*	p	4

This threat is not really strong enough to force a reply on the part of Black, and 141.c5* would now have been the strongest continuation, threatening to win the corner if White does not win the Ko.

141.	p	5	d	7*
143.	e	8		

Much stronger was e10, as indicated above.

143.	. . .		f	10
145.	s	9	s	12
147.	r	12	s	11
149.	s	10	r	11
151.	s	13	t	13
153.	t	14	p	13

White realizes that he cannot play t12, because 155.q 9 would follow with the double threat p13 and o8, the former attacking the ten White men on the right edge, and the latter saving the nine Black men, because o7 would be answered by 159.p7, capturing two men.

155.	q	9	o	8
157.	t	12*	t	11
159.	r	9		

Here Black had a good opportunity to play m7, n7, o7, and q7, netting him three or four points.

159.	. . .		q	7
161.	r	7	l	18
163.	m	18	g	18
165.	b	16	b	15

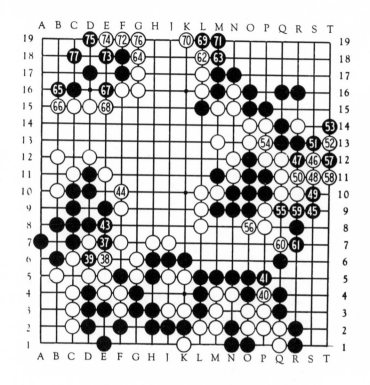

DIAGRAM 19

167.	e 16	e 15
169.	l 19	k 19
171.	m 19	f 19
173.	e 18	

Unnecessary. It was quite safe to play e 19.

173.	...	e 19
175.	d 19	g 19
177.	c 18	

If Black does not make this move, White can play c18 himself, and after Black protects with d18, he can continue with b17, and Black would lose the whole group.

177.	. . .	i 18
179.	g 8	

A very strong move, which wins four points by helping the man k6 to extend upward as far as k9.

179.	. . .	f 8
181.	g 7	f 6*
183.	k 7	i 8
185.	k 8	i 9
187.	k 9	k 10
189.	i 10	h 9

This reply was necessary and therefore it did not cost Black anything to sacrifice the man i10. He loses one man, but White had to reduce his own territory by one point.

191.	m 7	m 8
193.	n 7	n 8*9
195.	o 7	p 7
197.	p 6	l 7
199.	l 6	a 16
201.	a 17	a 15
203.	b 17	a 9
205.	a 8	a 5
207.	a 6	c 1
209.	d 1	b 9
211.	t 13	t 10
213.	t 9	d 6
215.	d 16	

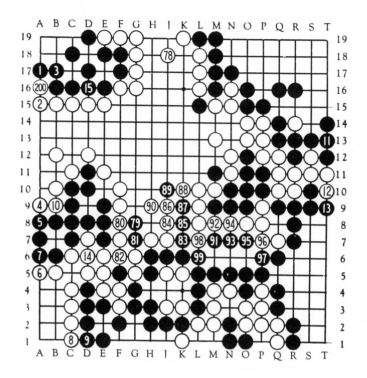

DIAGRAM 20

Now there are no more moves left which would win a point for one player or the other. The vacant points left between the Black and White chains are Dame. It does not matter who fills them in. There are only two of them, e10 and q8.

During the game Black has taken eleven prisoners and White has taken four. White now removes the five men g7, g8, i10, m11, and 1 15 from the board, making the total number of his prisoners 16, and Black removes r14 and the seventeen White men which he has caught near the lower edge, making the total number of his prisoners twenty-two.

After filling these twenty-two men into White's territory the latter has sixty-four points left, and after filling the seventeen Black prisoners into the Black territory there are seventy-seven points left, resulting in a victory for Black by thirteen points.

Every phase of the game has now been sufficiently discussed to save the student a great deal of time he would otherwise have to spend on finding out empirically the fundamentals of Go tactics. However, the beginner will find it rather difficult to keep the picture of the whole board before him clearly. He will lose himself in combinations concerned with a small part of the board rather than subordinating all of his manœuvres to a leading plan which takes in the whole board.

The best plan is to start playing on the 8 line board referred to on page iv. It offers sufficient room to practice all tactical manoeuvres we have discussed. Strategic operations on a grand scale, however, as conducted by advanced players, require the use of the large regulation board. Playing on it will gradually develop the student's understanding of the subtle influence upon each other of stones placed widely apart on the board.

Games at odds   In the Introduction I have alluded to the fact that the game of Go lends itself readily to a method of handicapping stronger players which equalizes the chances of winning even when players of widely different strength oppose each other. This adds a great deal of interest which is lacking in our Occidental games when a strong player is paired with a player much below his class.

[78]

As mentioned on page xviii, the weaker player is permitted to put one or more stones on the board before his opponent plays. These handicap stones are always placed on the points marked on the board with small circles or dots on the intersections of the fourth, tenth, and sixteenth lines with lines d, k, and q, in the manner explained below.

When receiving a handicap of nine stones, the largest ever given to players who are not rank beginners, Black begins the game by placing a stone on every one of the above described handicap points. If a handicap of eight stones is given, the centre point is left vacant. If the handicap is seven stones, k4 and k16 are left unoccupied, and if it is six the centre point is also left vacant. In a game with five stones handicap k4, k16, d10, and q10 are left open, and if only four stones are given the centre point is again left unoccupied. In a handicap of three stones d4, q4, and q16 are occupied, and in a game with the smallest handicap, which is two stones, only d4 and q16 are covered.

If the weaker player merely receives the first move, he is at liberty to place his man anywhere he wants.

It is a rule of politeness in the Orient, which I have never been able to understand, not to place the first man in the right-hand corner of the opponent. Thus, Black will never play his first move near d16. He usually starts near q16. If he commences near q4, in his own right-hand corner, White is at liberty to play in that neighbourhood too, having been invited, so to speak, by Black to enter that corner.

An Oriental player who plays with a stranger for the first time will always offer him the White men, as a gesture of politeness, to indicate that he considers himself the weaker player and is therefore satisfied to be given the advantage of the first move.

After the first game, if he wins, he will offer a handicap of a stone for about every ten points by which his score exceeded that of his opponent.

In the sample game which follows, Black receives a handicap of three stones. Small as this may look to a beginner, it is actually about the same as Knight odds in Chess.

White: Lieutenant Colonel Seisaburo Kinoshita
Black: Edward Lasker

Black has a handicap of three stones.

Black	White
1. d4, q4, q16	d15

This move is played too far out to secure a strong influence on the corner. White's plan is to play d17 next, unless Black occupies that point, and if Black does occupy it he wants to confine him in the corner and gain a strong base on the outside from which to extend toward k17 and c10, similar to the play discussed in connection with the position in the lower right corner of Diagram 17.

3. d 17	f 16
5. f 17	

Here, as well as on Black's next move, c15 would be stronger, because it would encircle more corner territory. White would not be able to cut this man off with c16, because after 7.d16, c14; 9.b15, b16; 11.b14, White must first guard against the immediate threat d14, and this gives Black time to play c17, winning the two White men, who have only two breathing-spaces, while Black's three men have three.

5. . . .	g 16
7. c 16	c 15
9. n 17	

Better would have been first g17, because if then White cuts

[80]

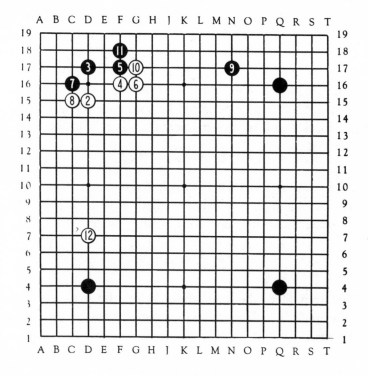

DIAGRAM 21

off the further development of this chain by h17, Black need no longer fear an attack against the corner, while without g17 the Black men are still somewhat loose and, as will be seen later, give White a chance to attack the corner.

$$
\begin{array}{llll}
9. & \cdots & \text{g 17} \\
11. & \text{f 18} & \text{d 7}
\end{array}
$$

This move has a double meaning. On one hand it threatens to place a man somewhere in the neighbourhood of d4, either on f4 or f3 or g3, thus making it difficult for Black's man on d4 to develop a position controlling much corner territory; and on the other hand it prepares the formation, at an opportune moment, of a position between the seventh and the tenth line which, in conjunction with the base formed by the White men on c15, d15, f16, and g16, would be a menace for any group which Black might try to settle near the left edge of the board.

13. g 3   o 3

The next seven moves, with which White forms territory between lines k and p near the lower edge and Black in the lower right corner, constitute an often recurring Joseki.

15. o 4   n 4
17. o 5

This strengthens the man whom White threatens to attack with o5, and also gains a move for extension toward the centre of the board.

17. ...   p 3

This strengthens the man on o3 and threatens an advance into Black's corner, thus maintaining Sente.

19. q 3   k 3

It would be premature to cut the Black group with p4; 21.p5, q5. The result would be the position which is mirrored in the lower left corner of Diagram 13.

21. q 6

[82]

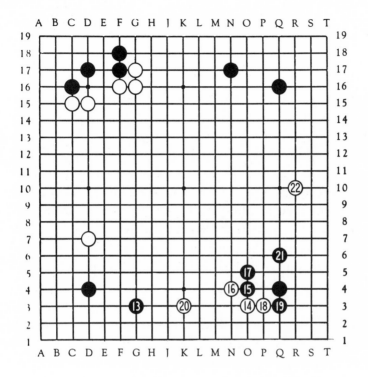

DIAGRAM 22

This secures a large corner and prevents the cut just alluded to at some later time.

21.   . . .   r 10

This play prepares a position in either the lower or the upper

half of the board on line r, depending upon where Black places
his next man.

$$23. \quad \text{r} \; 8 \qquad\qquad \text{r} \; 14$$
$$25. \quad \text{r} \; 16$$

Without this protecting move White might use the first opportunity to advance into this corner with s17, which would
connect with r14.

$$25. \quad \cdots \qquad\qquad \text{o} \; 14$$

This man may later prove useful for a connection with the
upper left corner as well as for an invasion into Black's territory
which would begin with p17, threatening either to form a safe
group in the corner or, if prevented by q17 or q18, to connect
with o14 via o16. The best answer for Black would be 27. n15
which would make both of these plans difficult to execute.

$$27. \quad \text{f} \; 5$$

A very weak move. If Black wants to strengthen his position
in this corner, he should do so with a man on c4 or c5 which
would effectively separate White's man on d7 from the corner
and prepare the formation of a settlement around d10, leaving
d10 somewhat hanging in the air.

$$27. \quad \cdots \qquad\qquad \text{f} \; 7$$

Now White's man is strengthened, and the plan just sketched
is much more difficult to execute.

$$29. \quad \text{c} \; 9 \qquad\qquad \text{c} \; 11$$
$$31. \quad \text{c} \; 7$$

This man cannot connect with d4, while this connection
would have been easy with a man on c5, as suggested in the note

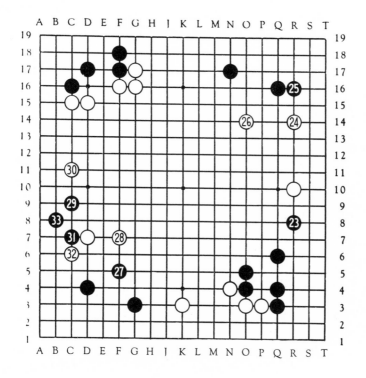

DIAGRAM 23

to the 27th move. Better, therefore, would have been e9, extending toward the centre.

| 31. | ... | c 6 |
| 33. | b 8 | |

Much better would have been d8. Black feared that White,

[85]

after d7 and perhaps 35.d9, could then connect with c11 through b7; 37.c8, a10. However, he would have been able to prevent this connection with 39. b8, a8; 41.b6, a7; 43. a9, b8*; 45. a6, and White cannot play a9 because 47.b10 would win the six White men. 33. d8 would have secured access to the middle of the board for Black, thus keeping the three White men c6, d7, and d9 hanging between two Black groups.

33.	. . .	b	7
35.	c 8	d	5

White now invades the corner while Black forms eyes for his group around d8, and in that way the Black group d4, f5, g3 is sandwiched between two White groups and must look for Me. Had Black played c5 instead of f5 on the 27th move, White would not have been able to embark on this favourable line of play.

37.	b 6	b	5
39.	a 7*	c	4
41.	d 3	c	3
43.	e 9		

It was much more important to do something for the group on the lower left, which has not yet formed clear outlines ensuring two Me. A good move would have been i4, threatening to invade the territory of the White group on the lower right, and after k4; 45.i5, k5; 47.k6, the Black group would have been out in the open, at the same time still pressing on the White group at the right. The move e9 was not urgent until White played b10, destroying the second eye of the group which Black could form by occupying that spot.

43.	. . .	e	4
45.	e 3	f	4

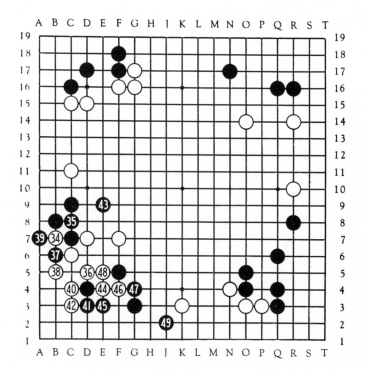

DIAGRAM 24

47. g 4   e 5

The Black group is now forced to fight for Me.

49.   i 2

i3 would have been better because it secures more clearly territory for Me.

[87]

49.	...	i	3
51.	h	3	

Here, however, h2 would have been better because it would have strengthened i2, which is now open to attack through k2.

51.	...	g	5
53.	k	2	1	2
55.	h	5	g	6

This is, of course, better than f6, because f5 cannot run away and the g6 strengthens g5.

57.	d	2	f	3
59.	f	2	c	2
61.	e	1		

Necessary because d1 threatened to destroy the eye on e2.

61.	...	1	17

This is over-aggressive. White wants to stake off huge territory in the centre; but he should first have strengthened the group on the lower right with k5, to guard against the cut at l 3 with which Black now gains the upper hand again.

63.	1	3	k	5

Too late. Comparatively best would have been l 4; 65. m3, m4; 67. m2, n3, pulling the men o3 and p3 out into the centre and cutting down the territorial gain of Black.

65.	1	4		

This is much stronger than m2, which White would have answered with l 4 and m4. The threat is now 67. k4, i4; 69.i5, etc.

65.	...	i	5

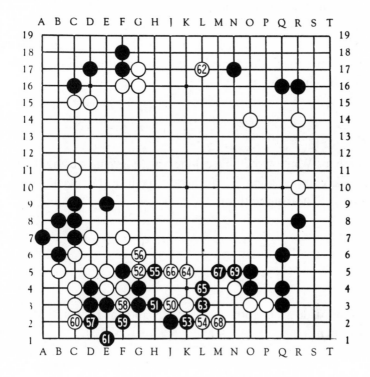

DIAGRAM 25

67. m 5

1 5, which would have threatened both the four men on the
right and the four men on the left, would have been stronger.

67. ...   m 2
69. n 5

[89]

Much better would have been q2, making it impossible for White to extend toward the corner and thus to gain some more space, which might be sufficient to form eyes in. Black need not have feared White's n5, as n6 would have shut off the White group effectively. There was no time for White to continue with m6, because Black threatened to win the two men on n4 and n5 immediately with n3.

| 69. | ... | q | 2 |

Perhaps White would have done best to give up this fight and to seek compensation by an attack against the Black group around c8, starting with b10.

71.	r	2	q	1
73.	o	1	o	2
75.	n	1		

Now p1 does not form an eye for White, as r1 would attack three men.

| 75. | ... | k | 1 |

Threatens h2.

| 77. | h | 2 | m | 4 |
| 79. | l | 5 | m | 3 |

Black has no difficulty in preventing the formation of two Me.

| 81. | r | 1 | p | 2 |
| 83. | n | 2 | | |

[90]

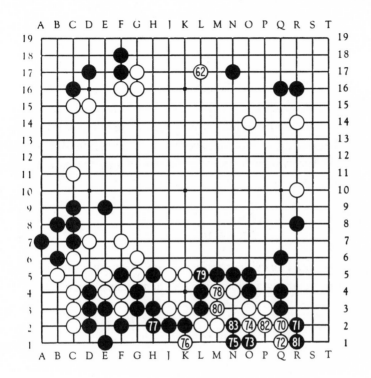

DIAGRAM 26

This kills White's group. He could have produced Seki with 84.l1, had the two halves of his chain been solidly connected by a man of his own at o4. As it is, however, the cut possible at n3 is fatal. It would not help White to occupy that spot himself, because the shape of the territory surrounded would then not lead to Seki. Black would sacrifice four men forming a

[91]

triangle by playing m1 and win as illustrated in Diagram 12 around k19.

83. ...   b 10

85. d 11

Black will have no difficulty in forming a second eye in the middle of the board, no matter in which direction he extends, because there are no White groups very close which could press him. A good move would have been g9, invading the centre, where White wants to develop his army from the base in the lower left quarter.

85. ...   d 12

87. c 10

Very weak. The evident reply was e11, strengthening the man on d11 and gaining a wider base for the invasion of the centre.

87. ...   e 11

89. d 10   b 12

Guarding against a cut into the territory on the upper left.

91. d 8

Again, g9 would have been much stronger. With d8 Black secures the second eye, but his group is shut off from the centre, where it could have decreased White's sphere of influence. All the eleven men composing Black's group have accomplished is adding two points to Black's total score.

91. ...   f 9

93. h 6

[92]

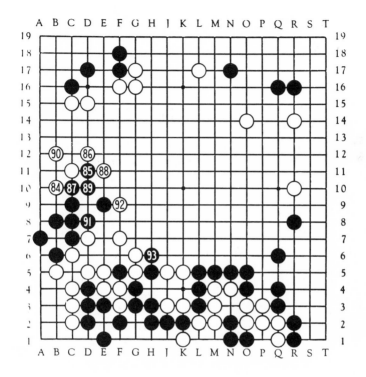

DIAGRAM 27

White can shut off the access to the centre of this man and the group led by it, and it would therefore have been better for Black to play 18 or 19 following this up with p9 or q9 and thus staking off large territory in the right centre. He might also have played n15, invading the centre from above and keeping the White men on the right side insecure.

[93]

93.	. . .	h	7
95.	i 6	i	7
97.	k 6	l	8

All Black has accomplished with his last three moves is the capture of four men, who, together with the territory involved, increase his score by about ten points, while White, with the same number of moves, has secured two or three times as much, since it is practically impossible for Black now to invade the territory between the eighth and sixteenth lines on the left side of the board without risking the loss of the whole invading force.

99.	n 9	m	10
101.	n 10	n	11
103.	m 9	l	9
105.	m 11	l	10
107.	o 11	n	12
109.	o 12	o	13
111.	o 15	n	15
113.	o 16	n	16
115.	p 15	p	14
117.	q 13		

This man can be cut off from o12, though in that case he can connect with p15 via q14. This plan would have been all right if the Black group extending from o12 to l 9 had been safe, as Black thought it was. However, White shows that there is still a chance to cut off this whole group. The best move was q 12.

117.	. . .	p	12
119.	p 11	q	12
121.	q 14	q	11
123.	r 13		

[94]

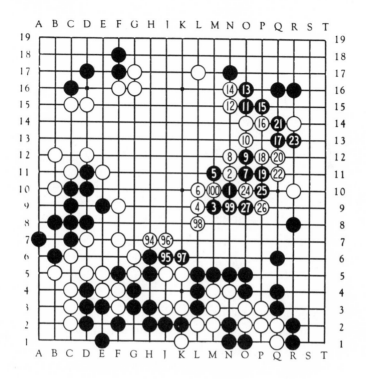

DIAGRAM 28

A bad blunder. Black does not yet realize that his group of six men is in immediate danger. At this moment p9 was necessary and if White connected at r13, Black could continue with 125.m16, threatening 127. n14, m15; 129. n13, p13; 131. m12, capturing two men. White would have therefore had to play 126.m14, but even then Black had many threats after first ex-

[95]

tending with 127.l 16. If White cut him off with m17, the consequence might have been 129.n13, m12; 131. m13, l 12; 133. l 13,
n14; 135. l 14, and the whole White army on the upper left was
cut off. On the other hand, if White played 128. n13, Black could
have connected at m17 or played k17 and gained access to the
middle of the board via k15, cutting into White's territory.

123.	. . .	o 10
125.	p 10	p 9
127.	o 9*	q 10
129.	o 10	p 8

The position arrived at now is very similar to the example
given in Diagram 4 around o9. There is no way for Black to
save his group.

| 131. | m 17 | l 16 |
| 133. | m 16 | m 15 |

Here both players overlook the combination with which Black
could now easily win the game. Beginning again with 135. n13,
Black would have captured the men m15, n15, and n16 and then
developed his group deep into White's territory: 136.m12;
137.m13, l12; 139. n14, p13; 141.l 15, etc.

| 135. | l 15 | m 13 |

The game is now practically over, because it is clear of all contestable territory to whom it belongs. The lower left corner,
worth about ten points together with the small territory comprised by this group on the sixth line, is in White's hands. White
also controls a large centre territory worth about seventy points;
and the right centre, where White has captured nine men, will
yield approximately another twenty points, making a total of a
hundred points.

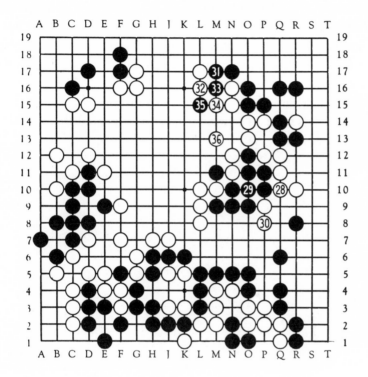

DIAGRAM 29

Black has secured about thirty points in the upper right corner, about fifteen points in the upper left corner and on the left edge of the board, about twenty points in the lower right corner, and about forty-five points on the lower edge, where he has captured sixteen men, yielding thirty-two points, and where another thirteen vacant points are comprised in the same chain.

[97]

This makes a total of ten points by which Black should win the game if both players share equally in the few points which are to be gained here and there in the end game. This end game has been discussed in detail on page 71, from which Diagram 29 is reproduced. The final result reached is indeed very close to the above estimate.

The fact that Black wins the game in spite of his many bad plays shows what an enormous advantage is entailed in the odds of three men.

« 3 »
BASIC
STRATEGY

W HEN TWO PLAYERS OF EQUAL SKILL are opposed in a game of Go, the outcome is very likely to depend upon the position reached after the first fifteen or twenty stones have been placed on either side. This statement will seem incredible to the beginner, to whom the vacant board appears to offer such a vast number of possibilities to start the game and to form living groups that twenty or thirty moves out of possibly two or three hundred which make up a whole game should be of insignificant importance.

All the same it is true of Go as it is of Chess and of simpler games such as Bridge or Checkers or Backgammon, that the game is usually won or lost in the opening, for any mistake made in the first few rounds of play is likely to leave an irretrievable weakness in the position.

It is not difficult to understand that this should be so in the simpler and shorter games just mentioned. That it is so in Chess even players of many years of experience rarely realize, because to them a game consists in a series of individual combinations which are only loosely connected, while in fact no combination, however ingenious, is likely to be sound unless it starts from a better position than that of the opponent, and forms part of a strategic plan which pervades the whole game and in which every man on the board plays his part.

The thorough grasp of this fact constitutes the difference between the average Chess-player and the expert, and it explains why an expert can play simultaneously against twenty, thirty, and more opponents and win the great majority of the games with ease. If it were not for the physical fatigue entailed in several hours of walking from board to board in an exhibition of simultaneous play, the expert would win every game, for usually he attains a winning position in the first ten or twelve moves, not because he sees farther than his opponents, but because he confines himself to making moves which he knows must be sound since they obey general strategic principles, while his adversaries, not knowing the application of these principles to Chess, are liable to make moves which are not sound and which lead them into a bad position. From a bad position it is rare enough for even an expert to emerge unbeaten. For the average player it is impossible unless his opponent makes a downright blunder.

The situation is very similar in the game of Go, although here the weaker player has several advantages which he lacks in Chess. The Go board is so much larger than the Chess board that a defeat on one wing of the battle-field can often be compensated by victory on another, particularly if the defending player succeeds in throwing a surrounded army into Ko.

Besides, the system of handicapping in Go makes possible so equitable a compensation for the difference in playing strength that an interesting battle is possible even between players of widely different experience.

As in Chess, the understanding of the application of general strategic principles is far more important in the game of Go than experience, as soon as a player has practised enough to see the traps and tactical threats typical of Go combinations which were discussed in the preceding chapter. It is strange that only comparatively recently the Oriental Go masters have realized how much easier it is to find one's way through the opening stage of a Go game by applying such general strategic principles than by memorizing opening methods which had been proved sound by many years of painstaking analysis. On the other hand, the same tardiness in the application of scientific thought can be observed in the development of our game of Chess. It was not until twenty-five or thirty years ago that Chess books began to teach the game by evolving general laws from the large number of cases which had been analysed during the preceding three or four centuries. Perhaps it is natural that the manner in which we play games should be a manifestation of the spirit of our time, like the manner in which we react to music or art or even business. To imagine Chess masters of fifty years ago playing a game in the style of today is as impossible as to think of Brahms composing in the manner of Stravinsky or Prokofieff.

Several of the young Go masters who are presently among the strongest players in Japan are working on books dealing with the strategy of Go, mainly in the opening phase, called "Fuseki" in Japanese, which comprises the first thirty or forty moves of a game. Born in this age of scientific thought, what they will say in their books will, I am sure, make obsolete most writings of the Go masters of the last three centuries, who were all bred in the atmosphere of the ancient Go academy of the first Honinbo.

In trying to develop general laws from which to judge the merits or demerits of a move we will naturally use as starting-point of all considerations the main object of the game, to gain as much territory as possible. A stone can control territory only in conjunction with other stones with which a connected chain can be formed, completely surrounding that territory. A chain composed of a certain number of stones will surround the more territory the looser the connection of the individual members of the chain. As long as no hostile stones are in the neighbourhood which threaten to break the connection between two members of a chain, it will therefore be advantageous to leave that connection loose, and only when the adversary approaches it, will it be advisable to tighten it.

A premature tightening of the connection between the members of a chain is evidently a waste of time which the opponent can utilize to his advantage by sketching loosely the outlines of additional territory which might have been contested.

The size of the territory which we stake off is limited by the possibilities the opponent has to gain a safe foothold within the territory sketched. From what we have learned in the preceding chapter we know that a stone placed in the third line can successfully ward off a hostile stone entering below it on the second line, while a man on the fourth line is too far away from the edge to guard the space between himself and the edge unless there are friends in the neighbourhood on the third line or on the second line with whom he can effect a connection.

Forming safe bases in the corners It follows that in establishing a base for a position the safest line to start on is the third in case no friendly stones are near on the third line, and that a base formed on the fourth line will enable the opponent to creep into the space between the base and the edge unless an additional stone is placed on a lower line to prevent this.

A second consideration which governs the decision where to form an army base is the number of men required to produce Me in that base in case of an attack.

To form a safe eye in a corner requires a maximum of three stones, while on the side five stones may be required, and seven

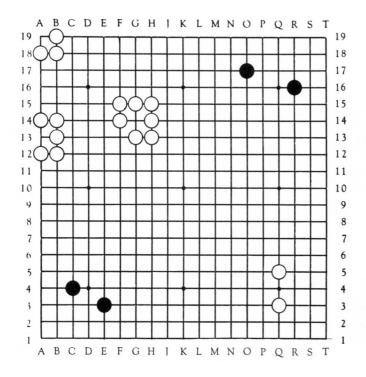

DIAGRAM 30

stones in the middle of the board, as illustrated in the upper left
of Diagram 30. We do not have to consider the number of stones
required to form two eyes here, because a group is safe enough
if it can form one eye as long as it maintains communication
with the centre of the board where it can connect with other
groups also containing one eye, and our considerations will soon

[103]

lead us to realize that this communication with the centre must be kept in mind whenever an army base is formed.

One thing is certain: to form at least one eye it will be best to start a group near a corner, because fewer moves are required there to produce that eye should the opponent attempt an attack, and since the only safe line to start on is the third, the number of moves which come into consideration is not large. In the lower left corner, for instance, only c3, c4, or c5 or the symmetrical points d3 and e3 could be chosen. Each one of these three different positions has its peculiar significance, a careful study of which will enormously advance the student's understanding of all strategic operations on the board, and which we will therefore discuss in detail.

At c3 a stone guards the corner without question most effectively, assuming as it were the role of two stones by defending roads of attack from the right as well as from above. However, on c3 a stone is less effective than on c4 or c5 from the second important viewpoint mentioned above, the ability to communicate with the centre of the board, where it might prove an aid to, or be aided by, a friendly group later on.

Of the two positions c4 and c5 the former has a stronger influence on the corner though it does not guarantee possession of it unless a second stone is placed on e3 or f3, to guard against an encroachment from the right.

On c4 a stone prevents the opponent from capturing the corner by occupying c3, because the answer would be 3.d3, c2; 5.d2, b4; 7.b5, c5; 9.d4, b6; 11.b3, a5*; 13.b2. Black would choose this defence only if he must form an eye in the corner because of pressure by White forces on the outside. In the beginning of the game the White attack would be very bad strategy because Black would permit the formation of a small White group in the corner and gain a much greater advantage by encircling

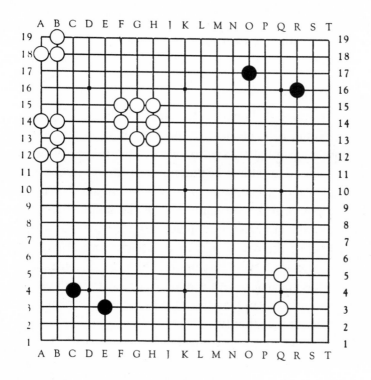

DIAGRAM 30

this group from the outside, cutting it off from the centre and obtaining a strong base for extension toward the right as well as the upper left, as follows: 7.c5, b5; 9.b6, b2; 11.d6.

After 1.c4 White will ordinarily start the formation of a base near another corner, and Black can then fortify his own corner by 3. e3 or e4 or f3, thus carrying out the original plan to secure enough space for one eye in the corner and at the same time to prepare the development of the base toward the sides and the centre.

The formation c4–e3 is the safest of the three, because it not only defends the corner against attacks from the sides but makes a separation of the two stones through an attack from the centre very difficult.

The formation shown in the upper right of Diagram 30, which would be equivalent to the position c4–f3, also defends the corner against attacks from the sides, but makes the position more liable to an attack beginning with the separation of the two stones at q17, as illustrated later. The position shown in the lower right, which is an equivalent of the position c4–e4, presents a solid front against an attack from the left, but does not securely close the corner against an attack from above. However, the opportunity to develop this formation by an extension toward the upper left with a stone placed at r7 or r8 often results in securing a larger corner territory with this opening than with either of the other two forms.

When extending the formation c4–e3 or r16–o17 toward the side of the board, it is easily understood that the extension should be made toward c10 rather than toward k3 and toward r10 rather than toward k17. For when the chain sketched by c4–e3 is substantiated by actual connection, a stone at c10 will have a wider base to support it than a stone at k3, and when the chain in the upper right corner is rigidly connected, a stone at r10 will have a wider base than a stone at k17.

A good practical rule as to how far one may extend from a base without danger of interception by the opponent is to jump one more space (on the third line) than the width of the base. In Diagram 31, for instance, we see a jump of four spaces to c9 from the base c4, d4, e4. If White plays c8, the development

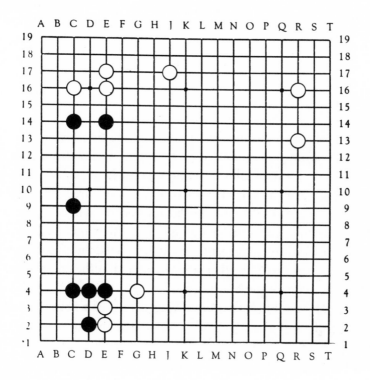

DIAGRAM 31

might be: 3. d8, d7; 5. c7, c6; 7. b8*, b7; 9. e7, c8*; 11.d6, c7; 13.b9, e8; 15.d9, e6; 17.f7, d5*; 19.f6, and the White group will die.

From e16–e17 White has extended as far as i17. If Black tries to separate the White men, perhaps with 1.g17, he will not succeed. For instance: g16; 3.h17, h16; 5. i18, k18; 7.k17, i16; 9. l 18, h 18; 11. k19*, g18.

These examples will suffice to demonstrate that, as we should naturally expect, the sphere of influence of one stone is smaller than that of two stones in a row, that the latter again is smaller than that of three stones in a row, etc. During the early stage of a game we have usually to weigh only the spheres of influence of single stones, because the connections between stones of the same colour are never substantiated unless an attack makes a tightening of the links of a chain necessary.

The influence or value of a stone after the first few opening moves is a function of what we might term its mobility. Near a corner a stone can usually be developed only in one or two directions, and near the side of the board in two or three directions, while near the middle of the board a stone will frequently have the choice between extending in four directions. The stone has more mobility in the centre because its freedom of extension is not yet hampered by other stones scattered in the corners and along the edges of the board.

Though the direct territory-taking ability of a stone in the middle of the board is much smaller than that of a stone in the third or fourth line, its indirect effect upon the size of the territory secured by the stones on the lower lines may be very great, because by means of stones in the middle of the board two or more chains may be united which comprised only one eye each, or perhaps not any, and so it will happen that weak chains, which had a hard time fighting for their lives, will suddenly be transformed into strong armies which can turn about and attack and perhaps capture their pursuers.

Since the potential sphere of influence of every stone extends in several directions, it is bad strategy to form a group in a corner or along the edge in a manner which enables the opponent to cut it off from the centre. Even if such a group embraces considerable territory, this is rarely a compensation for the disadvantages that the cut-off group cannot aid others by connecting with them and that the opponent obtains greater freedom of action in the centre, where he is no longer hampered by men emanating from that group.

The subject of a group's sphere of influence is closely related *The economical use of men* to another important subject, that of the economical use of men. Stones should not be so placed that their spheres of influence overlap, because this would be equivalent to a duplication of efforts, and it is very likely that an advantage is lost at another part of the board where the sphere of influence of the player in question might have been widened.

In Diagram 31, for instance, White, on the move, would play q3 rather than r4, because after developing r4 into a base formation in conjunction with a stone on o3 or p3 the logical side-extension would be at r9; or, if Black contests the corner by playing p3 himself, White would extend from r4 to r7, and in either case he would have a position on line r with a sphere of influence extending upward on lines r, s, and t, indicating the influence of the position r13–r16, which acts in the same sphere.

After placing a man on q3 White can extend to q5 if Black plays somewhere near the lower edge of the board; and if Black contests the corner with r5 instead, White can answer n3.

This would not lead to a duplication of efforts, for the position q3–n3 gives White a strong influence on the first three lines of the board, on which, due to the higher position of g4, he is not yet well established; and in the other variation the position q3–q5, which tends toward the middle of the board, would well balance the position r13–r16, which acts more along the edge. From the law of economical use of men, which needs no explanation, it follows without difficulty in many cases whether an intended formation of men is advantageous or disadvantageous. This holds not only of positional problems in the beginning of the game but also of tactical questions which arise in a hand to hand fight.

The application to positional problems suggests that whenever possible a stone should be so placed that both aggressive as well as defensive purposes are served. When a move is made to expand a safe position, or to defend it against a threatening invasion, that move should preferably also exert a threat against a hostile group. The use of men merely to secure two eyes within a position surrounded by the opponent is quite obviously uneconomical, and situations leading to such positions should be avoided unless the adversary has to make a comparable number of uneconomical moves to prevent the oppressed group from breaking out. The best way of avoiding the necessity to form two Me has been alluded to. It consists in maintaining communication with the centre. Not only does this entail the obvious advantage to weak chains that they will be able to connect with kindred men, thus avoiding the need for two Me within themselves, but it is also most desirable for strong groups, because the activity of a strong group is much more threatening, and thus more apt to gain additional territory than that of a weak one.

A position staked off in a corner with two men, as in the examples of Diagram 30, unless squeezed by hostile men from both sides, is ordinarily first expanded sideways before an extension is made toward the centre. The reason is that moves along the third or fourth line from the edge add much more potential territory to a group than can be expected from a move into the centre.

In a hand to hand fight the application of the law of economical use of men or effort will demand again that whenever possible a defensive move should at the same time carry the germ of a threat, and above all it will condemn any formations comprising more stones than necessary to obtain the desired effect.

Thus, in the lower left corner of Diagram 32, White, on the

[110]

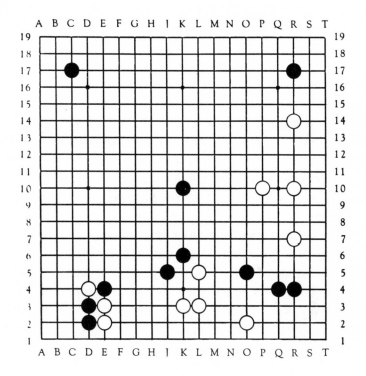

DIAGRAM 32

move, will play d2 before making any other move to develop his two men e3 and e4, because d2 not only helps those two men in forming Me but also attacks the two Black men d3 and d4 by reducing the number of free points to which they are connected.

If it were Black's move and he played m4, threatening to cut the connection between l3 and l5, White would not defend himself with the obvious move l4, but he would play k5. For this not only maintains the connection between his men on the third and fifth lines, but at the same time threatens the cut i6 which would lead to the capture of either k6 or l4 and result in a large territorial gain for White's group.

Extensions of the shape q4–o5, chosen by Black in the diagrammed position with the idea of playing l6, which would connect his corner group with his men in the lower centre, are of course more vulnerable to cuts than diagonal connections like i5–k6. The immediate cut 1.p5, p4; 3.o4, or 1.p4, p5; 3.q5 would not work. White's man on the fifth line would be attacked with p6 (q6) and could not escape. But after a preliminary move, such as 1.s5, for example, the above cut would be threatened. The safest extension toward the centre consists of a straight line jump skipping one point, as l3-l5 in the Diagram.

It is evident that communication of two groups located on different parts of the board via the centre with extensions of the type just referred to will be easier for that player who first places a stone near the centre, and since such a line of communication strengthens two weak groups, it will constitute an advantage over the opponent who must either leave two corresponding groups weak or strengthen them at the expense of one or more moves in each chain.

The question therefore arises whether the best plan is really to play first near a corner or whether Black should use his birthright of the first move to occupy a point in the centre.

All we can say is that very likely it is better to start near a corner because there a stone actually performs a tangible task by securing territory, while a stone in the centre does not perform the duty of connecting groups as long as no groups are as yet in existence.

The most modern games played in Japanese tournaments show sometimes occupation of a point in the centre as early as

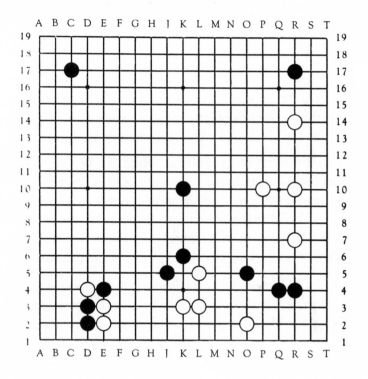

DIAGRAM 32

on the third move (the strategy of the great Chinese master), after two stones have occupied adjoining corners as shown in the diagram. The idea is possibly this: Ordinarily two stones are needed to form a position with one eye in a corner. If a move is spent to occupy a point in the centre, there would not be time to secure a corner as quickly as the opponent does it with such formations as those illustrated in Diagram 30. Therefore it is preferable to be satisfied with the much smaller corner territory that can be secured with one stone alone. As explained on page 104, this can be done only by occupying the intersection of the third lines.

Even game
Joseki Let us now examine in what way a player can dispute the possession of a corner with an opponent who has placed the first stone in that corner at a point which, in conjunction with a second stone, would produce one of the standard base formations.

Since the control of the point at which the two third lines intersect is the idea underlying every one of the base formations, attacks against the corner will be most effective which threaten the occupation of that point without helping the first player to strengthen his position with natural defensive moves to such an extent that the attacking stones themselves are weakened.

Diagram 33 shows four methods in which an advance against a base formation in the making may be started. It is assumed in every case that Black has placed his first stone at the intersection of the third and fourth line, which, as stated earlier, secures the strongest hold on the corner.

In each of the four cases the White move will be justifiable from the viewpoint of economy only if in addition to an attack against the corner it prepares an extension toward the side securing territory approximately equivalent to that which Black might take by immediately placing a second stone in the corner to prevent a further advance against it by White.

Black will place a second stone in the corner in question, rather than take a foothold in another corner, only if White threatens, by immediate occupation of the intersection of the third lines, to gain control of the larger part of the corner and

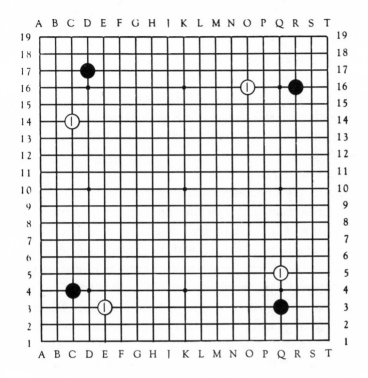

DIAGRAM 33

establish a strong influence at the same time toward the side from which he started the advance.

The same considerations by which we arrive at the proper line of play in the examples selected in Diagram 33 guide sound strategy in all openings, and the careful study of these examples will therefore advance the student further than memorizing a great variety of Joseki or analysed lines of play in corners, which fill the Japanese books on Go.

In the lower left corner White has placed a stone on the intersection of the third and fifth lines. If Black immediately fortifies the corner by embracing the intersection of the third lines with d3, the play ensues which we discussed in connection with the position in the lower right of Diagram 17. White would continue with 3. e4, and after 4. d6,5.i3 each player has a sound base for a chain which can freely develop toward the side and the centre.

What interests us here particularly is whether Black is really forced to reply to e3 immediately or whether he can play elsewhere. If he does, and if White continues his advance against the corner with 3. c3, Black will stop him with 4. b3; and after White strengthens his outpost with 5.d3, Black will play 6.b5 so that he does not have to make another move in protection of his corner outpost b3 later on, in case White plays b2 at any time.

High and low positions The position now arrived at is shown in Diagram 34. It cannot be considered good for White, for two reasons. One is that White has spent a move to substantiate the connection between c3 and e3 at an early stage of the game, a procedure which we recognized in our earlier discussions as uneconomical. The second is that White's men form a low position, being all located on the third line, while a stone on the fourth line is required for economical communication with the centre.

It might be argued that Black's men, too, have a low position. However, Black needs only one more move to form one Me while White needs two. For instance, if at some later time Black should have a stone on i3 as a result of the formation of a position on the lower right of the board, he would be threatening, by an extension to f2, to destroy the eye which White should be sure

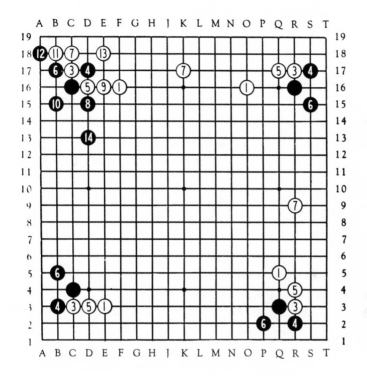

DIAGRAM 34

of below his men on c3, d3, and e3 in order to have any excuse
for that formation.

For these reasons Black can neglect to answer White's play at
e3 without fearing to be put at a disadvantage in this corner. If
base formations have already been established in the other three

corners, it is timely for Black to add a man to c4, either defensively on d5 or c7 or offensively at g3, h3, or i3. Before discussing these various possibilities in detail, we will examine the other positions alluded to in connection with Diagram 33.

In the lower right White has approached Black's initial stone again with only one line intervening, but this time on the fourth instead of the third line. If Black neglects to reply immediately in this case, White obtains the advantage. For after 3.r3, r2; 5.r4, p2 (Diagram 34) White's position can easily be developed toward the upper right, and it can readily communicate with the centre. He could continue 7.r9, for instance, and Black, clearly, has no way to extend from his three men in this corner which will yield an equivalent territory.

White's advantage is still greater if Black permits him to occupy the intersection of the third lines after approaching the corner in the manner shown in the upper right of Diagrams 33 and 34, where two lines intervene between the two opposing men.

Obviously the continuation 3.r17, s17; 5.q17, s15; 7.k17, will yield three points more to White than the formation in the lower right, apart from extending the sphere of influence of the group upon any position the opponent may build up in the neighbouring quarter of the board.

Before we can state definitely that an advance against the corner as just sketched with White's first two moves is favourable, we would, of course, have to prove that Black cannot separate the two White men. If he does, play might proceed as illustrated in the upper left of Diagram 34. After neglecting to answer White's first move in this corner Black tries to stem White's advance 3.c17 with 4.d17, and White cuts with 5.d16. Quite generally speaking, it is likely that this hand to hand fight will result in White's favour because he has three men

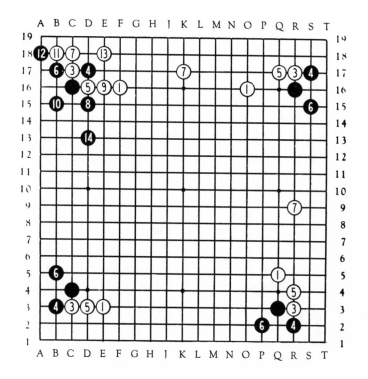

against two engaged in it. The result of the analysis confirms this prognosis.

After 6.b17; 7.b18, d15; 9.e16, Black must first guard his loose diagonal formation against cuts by playing 10.b15. This gives White time to save his two men c17 and c18, which a Black move to d18 would doom, by adding a breathing-space to them with 11. b18, threatening at the same time to weaken Black's group by killing its eye on b16 by playing a17. Black prevents this threat with 12.a18 without wasting a move, because White must again defend his two men c17 and c18 against the threat d18. However, 13.e18 accomplishes this without losing the advantage of Sente, because Black can hardly leave his position without placing another man as a guard against an attack which might start from c14. He will probably do best to continue with 14.d13, but even then his position is evidently weaker than White's, because it needs more stones to substantiate the formation of genuine eyes and is therefore more exposed to attacks, particularly in case of Ko fights.

In drawing our conclusions as to the advantage or disadvantage entailed in Black's or White's position in this corner fight as well as in any hand to hand fight in a corner which is discussed in standard openings, we must always keep in mind that the positions in neighbouring territories vitally affect these conclusions. Sometimes neighbouring positions will make an opening playable which would be disadvantageous if the position in the corner alone were the deciding factor.

In the example just discussed, for instance, Black might decide to let White make his attack if there were a Black man or two in the ninth or tenth line near the left edge, perhaps on c10 and e10. This is unlikely, because the corners are ordinarily disputed before the sides are invaded, but it might happen in games which from the start take a course out of the ordinary.

Out of considerations of this kind the play in the example just cited might have taken a different course at Black's or White's option. On the sixth move Black might have first cut at e16, as illustrated in Diagram 35. After 7. d15, e17, White can choose between taking the corner 9.c15 followed by 11.c17, which would permit Black to come out at e15, and shutting off

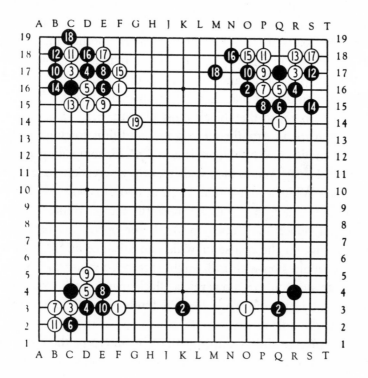

DIAGRAM 35

Black with 9.e15 and letting him have a small position in the corner, while White obtains a strong base for extension along the left edge as well as the upper right.

White will choose the former course if he has already established a position in the centre of the upper edge, because then the Black group developing from stones d17, e17, and e16 will have to fight its way between two strong opposing chains. He will confine Black in the corner if the sides flanking that corner are not yet developed. This alternative is illustrated in Diagram 35. After 9.e15, b17, White first sacrifices another man with 11.c18 because in this way he forces Black to make another three moves in the corner and he can complete the girdle around Black's men during that time. The immediate threat is b16 followed by b 18, so that Black must play 12. b18. Then follow 13. c15, b 16; 15. f17, threatening e18, and thus forcing 16.d18. A fine move on White's part is now 17. e18, compelling Black to take the two White men with 18. c19, whereupon 19. g14 or f14 gives White a tremendous front in two directions.

Without inserting this seventeenth move White would leave an opportunity open to Black for operations near the upper edge in the course of which an advance at f18, which White would stop with g18, might threaten a cut at g17. With a White stone at e18, however, a Black man on f18 would be attacked by g18, and while Black defends him White has time to close the hole at g17.

The unsuccessful attempt by Black to intercept the connection between stones 1 and 3 invites a comparison with the play which might arise from the constellation shown in the upper left of Diagram 33. Turned at an angle of ninety degrees, this constellation is repeated in the lower left of Diagram 35. If Black disregards White's first move and plays elsewhere, and White continues his advance against the corner with 3.c3, Black can intercept the connection with 4. d3; 5.d4, c2; 7. b3, e4; 9.d5, e3. There is no way for White to connect stone d5 with f3, shutting Black into the corner, as he was able to in the preceding example by connecting stone d15 with f17. He will therefore have to content himself with taking the better half of the corner by playing 11. b2, and Black might continue with d7 or e5.

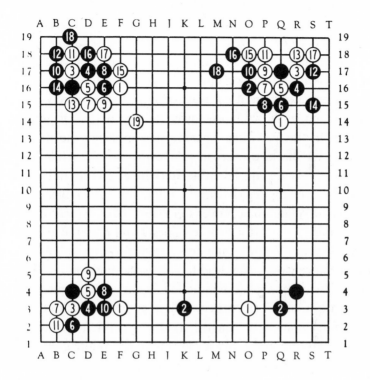

DIAGRAM 35

The latter move would be particularly effective if Black, foreseeing the development just sketched, had placed a man on k3 with his second move.

We conclude from this line of play that White's first stone at the intersection of the third and sixth lines, forming a sort of an extended Knight's move from Black's initial stone, is not as urgent a threat against the corner as a stone placed at the intersection of the fourth and sixth lines, or of the fourth and fifth lines, as illustrated in the examples of Diagram 34.

It remains to be seen, of course, which one of these moves is preferable when viewed from the positions resulting in case Black defends himself against White's advance, playing a man so that White cannot occupy the intersection of the two third lines. Such a man need not necessarily be placed closely to that intersection, as shown in the lower right corner of Diagram 35, though in this particular opening it is probably the strongest defence for Black, who secures the corner with it while White can hardly secure equivalent territory by extending to l3 or k3.

In the opening depicted in the upper left corner Black's best answer to White's first move is probably 2.d14, which prepares to embrace large space between lines a and c and at the same time prevents White's intended advance to c17 indirectly, as this advance would now lead to a very bad position for White. A possible line of play is indicated in the upper right corner. After 1.q14, o16; 3.r17, r16; 5. q16, q15; 7.p16, which produces the same position as reached in the upper left corner after White's seventh move, Black can shut in the White group completely with 8.p15, utilizing his second stone. The consequence might be 9.p17, o17; 11. p18, s17; 13.r18, s15, and White must still defend himself against the threats o18 and s18, which would kill his second Me. After 15.o18, n18; 17.s18, m17, White is completely shut in.

In passing, it might be pointed out that 11.q18, taking the Black man instead of playing p18 would have been just as bad for White, for 12.p18; 13.q17, s16; 15.o18, n18; 17.p19*, m17; 19.s17, r14, again shuts him in completely, with the result that he has secured only about six or eight points at the expense of ten moves, while Black, with his surrounding chain, has secured

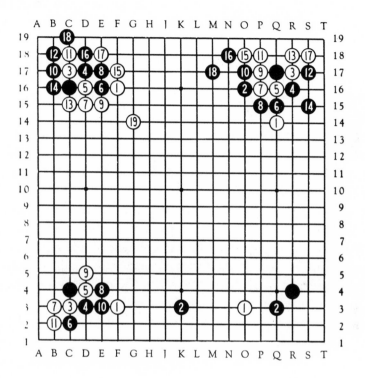

DIAGRAM 35

so large a sphere of influence that he is certain to gain control of large territory.

Diagram 36 shows how Black might defend himself in case White chooses the advance against the base in the corner illustrated in the lower right corner of Diagram 33.

Again Black can guard against the occupation of the inter-

[125]

section of the third lines and at the same time strike out for territory, and White will not be able to confine him in the corner by sacrificing two men in the manner described in connection with the position in the upper left corner of Diagram 35.

For instance: 1.q5, r5; 3. q4, r4; 5. r3, r2; 7. s3, s2; 9.p3, q2; 11. r6, s4; 13. s5, t3*2; 15. q7, o3, and Black connects stone 16 with q2, as 17.p2, o2; 19. p1 cannot be played on account of 20. p4.

If instead of playing q7 White shuts the Black group in with 15.o4, he is liable to get into trouble later on through Black's cutting at q6, which separates the White men into two weak groups. Should a Black position be already established near the upper right edge as shown in the diagram, the cut at q6 would immediately place White in the most precarious situation, for after 17.q7, p6; 19.p7, o5, White would have to lose a move to protect himself against the threat p4, and Black continues with o7, whereupon White will surely lose one of his two groups. And if he plays 19. s7, p7; 21.q8, Black will again continue with o5, and after 23. p4, n4 the White army is again almost certain to perish. For instance: 25. n3, m4; 27. m3, l 3; 29. l 2, k2; 31. m2, k4; 33.o2,p2; 35. n1, l 1, or 33. p2, o2; 35.o1 n1; 37. p1, n2, and there is only one Me.

The position in the upper right is an example of the development which might take place if instead of occupying the intersection of the third lines the player who has prepared that advance on the corner desists from it after the opponent has made a defensive move, and is satisfied to seek compensation on the side of the board. The result is, naturally, in favour of the player who has placed the initial stone near the corner.

Another example is shown in the upper left. Play might have ceased there for the time being after White has placed stone 5,

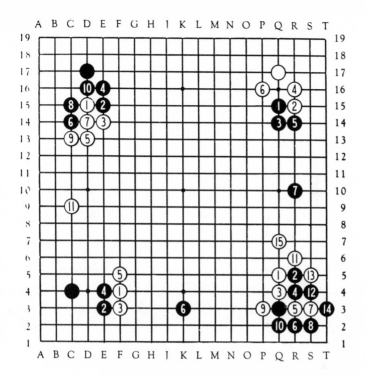

DIAGRAM 36

to be resumed at an opportune moment later, when neighbouring positions have come into being which might suggest either
the line of play shown in the diagram or somewhat different
variations. The same holds of a number of other examples given
in this chapter. The lines of play given always presuppose that
at the moment there is no more urgent task to be attended to at

another part of the board, and that there are no stones in the immediate neighbourhood of the scene of battle which might take a hand in it. Some of the attacks shown in previous examples as unsuccessful might be very good as soon as a group is formed in the neighbourhood of the scene in question with which a weak link in the attacking force might be able to connect. Thus the proper timing of an attack is almost always the factor which decides the outcome.

Also, since a hand to hand fight can usually be conducted in more than one way, and since neighbouring positions determine which is the best way, we are justified in formulating a strategic law which demands that hand to hand fights should be postponed until base formations have been sketched in corners and along the sides of the board.

Of course, this presupposes that both players play the opening fairly well. If one player makes a move which violates the general principles of strategy, thus giving his opponent a chance to gain a decided advantage by a hand to hand fight at a point where he would otherwise not have attacked, such attack can no longer be termed premature.

The positions on the left side of Diagram 36 illustrate strikingly the advantage of keeping the option of different lines of attack as long as possible. Let us assume that except for Black's initial stone at c4 no man has been placed as yet in the lower left corner. If Black stops playing in the upper left corner after White has placed the fifth stone there, he has the option to answer White's 1.f4 either with d6, as in the upper right of Diagram 35, which would prepare taking territory on the left with a further stone placed on c8 or c9, or with e3, which would start operations along the lower side of the board, possibly continuing, as indicated in Diagram 36, with 3.f3, e4; 5.f5. k3. The latter play will be favourable for Black only in case he has a strong base in the lower right which supports the stone at k3.

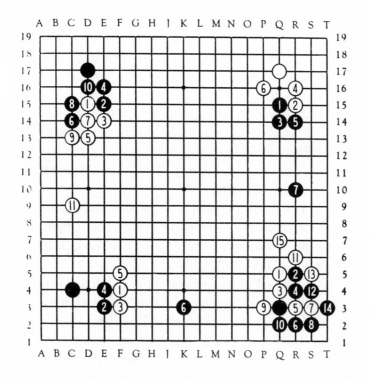

DIAGRAM 36

Otherwise he will prefer 2.d6. However, if Black has prematurely continued the play in the upper left corner with 6.c14, resulting in White's forming a position with an outpost at c9, the line of play in the lower corner beginning with 2.d6 has lost its strategic significance.

Even the line of play shown in Diagram 36 in the lower left, with the extension at k3 from a supposed strong base in the lower right, would be stronger for Black had he not prematurely advanced the situation in the upper left to a stage in which White arrives at a substantial base formation. For the three White men in line f, sandwiched as they are between two strong hostile groups, would have much greater difficulty in finding a haven of refuge if White did not have an outpost on c9.

The sandwiching of a weak group between two chains is one of the most important strategic manœuvres on the Go board. Though the weak group may often succeed in escaping or connecting with a kindred group at another part of the board, the two hostile chains, in pursuing it, often form a wall which secures a great deal of territory.

That is why in the opening a player should avoid invading space which is flanked by two hostile groups, unless these groups are still weak, so that they themselves are liable to be threatened by the growth of the invading chain.

Untimely cuts　In the middle game inexperienced players almost invariably get into all sorts of trouble through sandwiching attacks similar to those just described and which arise, as a rule, after a cut has been made with a stone that cannot be readily connected with a safe group. Such a cut is justifiable only if at least one of the two parts of the cut group is weak, so that it is almost as vulnerable as the chain which develops from the point of the cut. The following game offers a very instructive example.

Black receives the odds of three moves and accordingly occupies points d4, q4, and q16 at the start (Diagram 37).

Black   *White*

1. d4, q4, q16   c 16

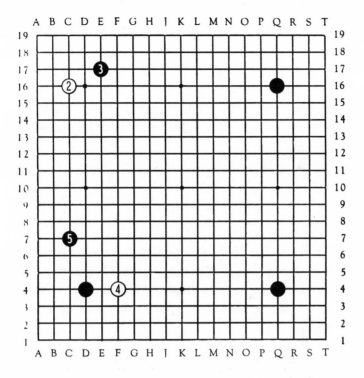

DIAGRAM 37

3   e 17   f 4

For reasons explained on page 116 White need not immediately reply to Black's advance upon his base in the upper corner. In answer to f4 Black places a man on the other side of the handicap stone so as to prevent the latter from being sandwiched between two White positions.

White wants the position which Black will develop from his stone e17 to extend on the upper edge rather than toward the position just formed on the lower left, because he wants his own position, which will start from stone c16, to maintain free access to the centre. If he played 6.h17 instead of e17, Black would reply e14, and the sphere of influence of the White corner position would be limited.

7.	f 16	e 15
9.	d 17	c 17
11.	i 17	o 17

If it were not for the fact that Black has such a tremendous advantage due to initial occupation of the other corners, White would here play c11 or c10, sketching a little more clearly the territory for which his other stones in that part of the board form a base.

13. r 13   l 17

After thus establishing a position on the right upper edge White threatens sooner or later to invade the upper right corner with a stone on r17 or r18, and so Black guards the entrance to this corner immediately. After he has placed a man on q17, he is practically certain that the corner territory will fall to him. It is important to note that it takes three stones to secure possession of a corner, two in addition to the stone on the handicap point, while ordinarily two stones are sufficient for this purpose, as explained in detail in this chapter. That is why in a game with three stones handicap White plays always first in the open corner, which he can secure with two men.

[132]

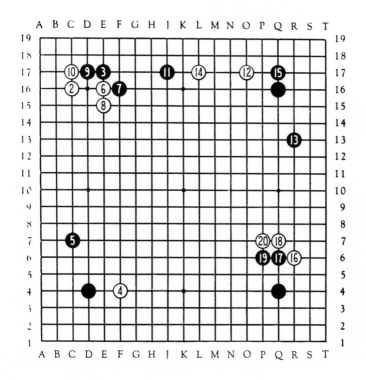

DIAGRAM 38

15. q 17	r 6
17. q 6	q 7
19. p 6	p 7

Generally r5 is played here, followed by r10, similar to Black's formation in the upper left.

White is now ready either to expand with r11 or to operate somewhere near the right lower edge, sandwiching the Black position. Black's best answer would be o4, securing large territory in the corner. If White continued with r11, Black could then play o7, whereupon White would have to build a position from his man on f4 with little prospect of connection with any other group of his.

23. r 10   o 3

Black opposes White's extension upward, and White immediately seizes the opportunity to establish himself on the lower edge, at the same time squeezing the Black corner position.

25. p 3   p 2

Black should now answer q2. The move he chooses leads to a disadvantageous formation, as discussed on page 111.

27. q 3   o 4
29. o 6   q 2

White has the hard decision to make whether to leave his position on the lower edge weak or the position on the seventh line. If he plays 30. o7, Black secures a large corner with q2, threatening at the same time to squeeze White with o2. To the move of the text Black should answer o7, pressing the upper White position. White could then hardly have played s3 on account of o10, which would make the formation of Me very difficult for White, if possible at all.

31. s 3   o 7

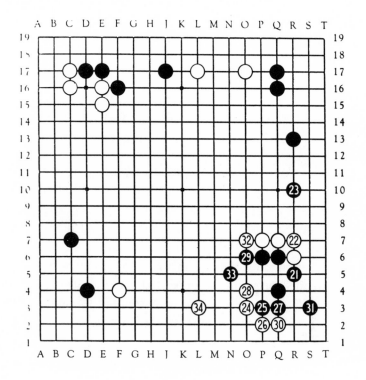

DIAGRAM 39

33. n 5   1 3

White forms a position on the lower edge because Black, with
his last move, threatened to attack the White group with m3.
Instead of n5 Black should have played m6, because that move
would have threatened White's lower group as well as that on

[135]

the seventh line. Had White answered o 10, Black could have continued with l 3, and it is doubtful whether White would have been able to form two Me. Even if he succeeded in barely saving his group, the fight would have resulted in a solid wall of Black men on lines l and m, making it exceedingly difficult for White to develop a position from his man on f4, which he would have to do in order not to let all territory in the lower left quarter of the board fall into Black's hands.

35. n 7   o 10

White seeks a connection with his position l 17–o 17. That position is as yet weak, since it is flanked by two Black positions, a very strong one in the corner and one on the upper edge which Black would now have time to strengthen and develop with 37. i 15. The continuation which Black chooses instead is very bad, because it is directed against a strong group with a weak stone. White's group in the upper left corner is strong because it can easily form one Me and it is communicating with the centre. Black's attacking stone on c14 is weak because it is not connectible to a strong group.

37. c 14   c 15
39. c 11   h 16

This "shoulder attack" is an often recurring method which should be carefully noted. If Black answers i16, White continues with h15, and if Black plays h17 instead, White replies g16. In either case White will establish connection with at least one of his groups on the upper edge and possibly with both, thus endangering Black's position in that region.

Black's best reply would now be f15, separating White's man from the stronger of the two groups with which he seeks connection and securing communication with the centre, at the

[136]

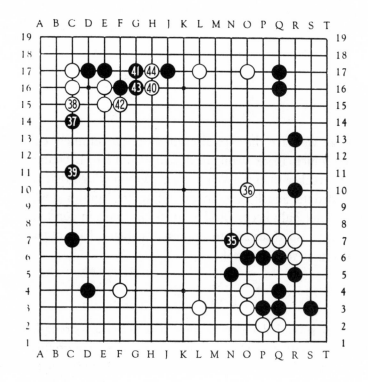

DIAGRAM 40

same time threatening to cut off from the centre the White corner group.

| 41. g 17 | f 15 |
| 43. g 16 | h 17 |

Immediately taking advantage of the undesirable formation

which Black has chosen (compare Diagram 27, page 111). Black must add another stone to the men f16,g16,g17 to guard against the attack g18, and White has time to shut off Black's group completely.

45. h 18	g 15
47. f 18	i 16
49. h 15	i 15

Here we have the typical example of an untimely cut. The chain which Black wants to develop from h15 is bound to be much weaker than the White corner group which that chain is intended to attack, and in extending that group downward White not only keeps Black's attacking chain in constant danger, but also threatens to oppress the Black base c14–c11–c7, which is as yet very weak.

| 51. h 14 | i 18 |
| 53. g 19 | e 12 |

Black should abandon his two men and either strengthen his left wing with c13 or, better still, expand his strong group on the right wing by p10, which would threaten to cut the line of communication between White's groups on the seventh line and on the upper edge.

55. e 13	c 12
57. b 12	c 13
59. b 13	d 14
61. i 14	l 15
63. f 13	b 14*

Now, this is important, because if Black plays b14, White needs a lot of moves to form Me in his group, and the Black men

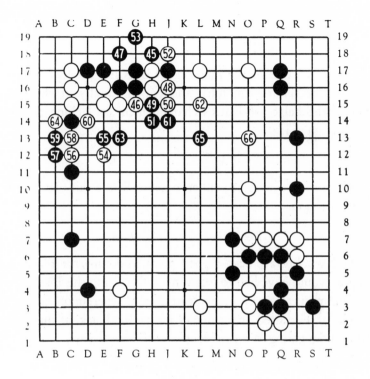

DIAGRAM 41

in the centre would endanger that group in working for their escape downward.

65. l 13   o 13

Wherever the Black chain tries to flee, White blocks the escape or cuts through its links where they are not solidly connected.

[139]

67. n 14	k 14
69. k 13	i 13
71. g 14	h 12
73. f 12	d 11
75. i 12	i 11

Black's capture of the man on i13 does not produce an eye because the White men on h12 and k14 will finally attack either one of the halves of Black's chain, which are lacking a solid connection at i13.

77. h 13*	g 11

There is no eye on g13 either, because White can play f14 in answer to g12.

79. f 11	o 14

This would have been a good point to occupy for Black, as White would have had to lose time with cutting the Black line of communication by m14; 81.n13, m13, whereupon 83. m12 might have secured an avenue of escape for Black, at the same time endangering White's group on the seventh line.

81. c 10	d 10
83. n 15	o 15

Black has managed to develop a dangerous attack which should help him to make sufficient elbow room to save his centre group.

85. o 16	n 16
87. m 16	n 17
89. m 17	m 15
91. m 18	l 18
93. o 18	p 16*
95. n 18	m 13

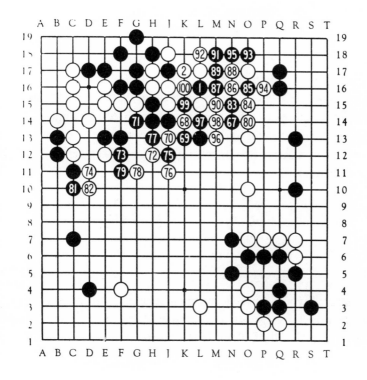

DIAGRAM 42

97. l 14	m 14
99. k 15*	k 16
101. l 16	k 17*

This is very dangerous and might have led to great loss for White, because the life of his chain now depends upon the Ko on k14–k15. He should have recaptured at k14. Black now destroys the second Me.

| 103. | k 19 | k 14 |
| 105. | p 17 | |

Very bad. Here was a splendid opportunity either to run away with the chain caught in the centre, by k11 for instance, or to make a Ko threat against the chain on the seventh line by p9. The move of the text threatens only three men, and White gladly sacrifices them and takes the opportunity to connect his chain at k15. After that Black's group in the centre is again in grave danger.

105.	...	k 15
107.	o 16*3	l 11
109.	f 9	d 8
111.	g 10	e 10
113.	f 10	i 9

Here c8 would have been much stronger, cutting the Black men on the left edge into two very weak groups, without losing the grip on the Black chain in the centre.

115.	e 8	d 7
117.	c 8	e 7
119.	e 9	d 9
121.	g 8	h 9

Again Black's effort to build a second Me is frustrated. After f7 the eye on f8 can always be made false through either g9 or g7.

123.	f 7	c 6
125.	e 5	f 5
127.	d 6	e 6

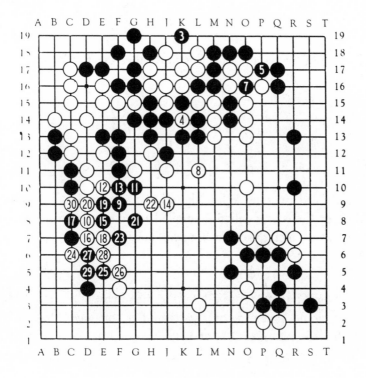

DIAGRAM 43

Possibly White had better stopped here to play b6, which would again have seriously endangered all Black men on the left wing.

129. d 5   c 9

Now Black gives up the four men above the ninth line, but

[143]

secures a large corner.

| 131. b 6 | b 7 |
| 133. c 5* | h 6 |

It seems fairly certain after this move that the Black group in the centre will perish.

135. h 7	i 7
137. g 6	h 5
139. g 5	g 4
141. h 4	h 8

But this is dangerous. White should play f6 in order to deprive Black of the counter-chance entailed in an attack on the men around f4, which the cut at f6 makes possible.

| 143. f 6 | g 7* |

If Black had to protect his four men which are attacked, White would have time to play h3 and i3, thus saving his men which were cut off at f6. But Black takes advantage of the Ko at g7–h7 to occupy h3, and he saves his whole army by capturing the small White group on lines f and g.

| 145. k 11 | h 11 |

The threat was i10 followed by h10, which would have given the Black chain the second eye without trouble.

147. h 7*	i 4
149. h 3	g 7*
151. f 8	g 3
153. h 2	g 2
155. k 2	i 2

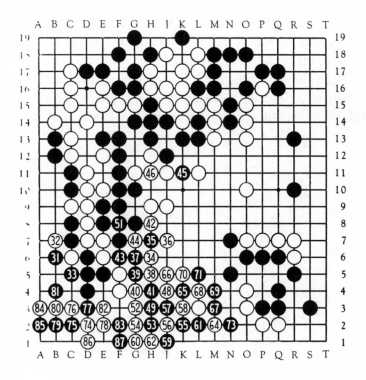

DIAGRAM 44

157. i 3   k 3
159. i 1*   g 1

Much simpler appears l 2, but this would have given Black an opportunity to produce a Ko at k1–i1, and White naturally tries to avoid that.

161.	l 2	h 1
163.	i 2	m 2

This terrible blunder deprives White of the fruit of all his labours. Had he played m3; 165.m2, n2, there would have been no escape for the Black group, and the whole centre army would no doubt also have been lost. As it is, White makes a last desperate attempt to win that army by saving his group around f4, and when that attempt fails, he resigns the hopeless game.

165.	k 4	i 5
167.	m 3	l 4
169.	m 4	k 5*
171.	l 5	k 4
173.	n 2	d 2
175.	c 2	c 3
177.	d 3	e 2
179.	b 2	b 3
181.	b 4	e 3
183.	f 2	a 3
185.	a 2	d 1
187.	f 1	White resigns

When Black receives odds of more than three stones, there is no good move for White to start the game, as Black has the advantage in all four corners. The methods of attacking the corners which are comparatively the best have been analysed and tested by many masters of the game. The table below gives a summary of the Joseki which are most frequently used. The strategic considerations given in this chapter will furnish a good guide for their understanding.

Black stone on d4. Odd-numbered moves are White's.

A. 1.f 3, c 7; 3.c 3, d 3; 5.c 4, c 2; 7.b 2, d 2; 9.c 5
B. 1. "   "   3. "   "   5. "   d 5; 7.d 2, e 2; 9.c 2, e 3; 11.b 6, c 6;
C. 1. "   "   3. "   "   5.d 2, e 2; 7.b 2, d 1; 9.c 2, e 3; 11.c 5
D. 1. "   "   3. "   "   5. "   "   7.c 2, e 3; 9.b 5, c 5; 11.c 4, c 6;
E. 1. "   "   3.c 9, d 3; 5.f 5, e 7; 7.e 9, g 7; 9.h 6, b 8;
F. 1. "   "   3. "   "   5.c 5, d 5; 7.c 6, d 7; 9.c 2, d 2; 11.b 3
G. 1. "   "   3.d 3, c 3; 5.c 4, d 5; 7.c 2, b 3; 9.e 2, b 2; 11.b 1
H. 1. "   "   3.f 5, i 3; 5.d 5, c 5; 7.c 4, c 3; 9.b 4, b 3; 11.b 5, c 6;
I. 1. "   "   3. " d 3; 5.c 5, d 6; 7.b 3
K. 1. "   f 4; 3.g 4, f 5; 5.e 3, d 3; 7.c 6, c 5; 9.d 7
L. 1. "   "   3. "   "   5. "   "   7.g 5, g 6; 9.d 2
M. 1. "   "   3. "   "   5.c 3, e 3; 7.c 4, c 6; 9.c 5
N. 1. "   "   3. "   "   5.d 3, e 3; 7.e 2, e 4; 9.g 2, c 3; 11.d 2, g 5;
O. 1. "   "   3. "   "   5.c 6, e 3; 7.g 3, b 5; 9.d 7, f 2;
P. 1. "   "   3. "   "   5. "   d 6; 7.c 5, c 4; 9.d 5, g 3; 11.e 3, e 4;
Q. 1. "   h 3; 3.f 5, h 5; 5.d 2
R. 1. "   "   3. " d 2; 5.e 2, h 5; 7.d 6, b 5;
S. 1. "   "   3.c 6, f 4; 5.e 4
T. 1. "   "   3.c 3, d 3; 5.c 4, c 2; 7.b 2, d 2; 9.c 6
U. 1. "   d 6; 3.c 8, i 3; 5.d 2, f 4; 7.e 3, g 4; 9.c 3, c 4; 11.e 8, d 3;
V. 1. "   c 10; 3.c 6, f 4; 5.g 4, f 5; 7.c 3, e 3; 9.g 3, c 4; 11.b 4, b 2;
W. 1.h 3, f 3; 3.c 6, c 5; 5.d 6, f 5; 7.f 6, h 4; 9.i 4, h 5; 11.g 3, f 2;
X. 1. "   "   3.b 5, b 4; 5.c 4, c 5; 7.c 3, b 3; 9.d 3, e 4; 11.b 6, c 2;
Y. 1.g 4, d 6; 3.c 8, k 3; 5.d 2, d 3; 7.f 2, c 2
Z. 1. "   f 3; 3.g 3, f 4; 5.f 5, g 2; 7.h 2, f 2; 9.h 5, g 6; 11.g 6, d 6;
AA. 1. "   d 7; 3.d 3, e 3; 5.e 4, c 3; 7.d 2, e 5; 9.f 4, c 4; 11.c 2, b 2;
BB. 1.f 4, d 6; 3.c 8, e 7; 5.d 10, h 3; 7.g 5, h 5; 9.h 6, h 4; 11.e 3, d 3;
CC. 1.f 4, f 3; 3.e 3, e 4; 5.g 3, f 2; 7.e 2, g 2; 9.c 3, c 4; 11.b 3, h 3;

Neither the handicap Joseki listed on the preceding page nor the even game Joseki discussed on pages 114 to 130 should be memorized. They should merely serve as examples of the way in which the strategic principles, which guide all operations on the board, may be applied in the opening stage of the game.

In good games, the Josekis employed in the different corners are by no means selected at random. The position in one corner often exerts a subtle influence on the play in another, something the student is apt to have considerable difficulty in grasping without properly guided experience. The following game, probably one of the most beautiful on record, may serve as an instructive illustration. It was played in 1926 by the then reigning champion, Honinbo Shusai, against the eighth rank master, Karigane, the leader of a rival organization.

Black: Karigane   White: Honinbo

1.	r 16	r	4
3.	p 16	d	17
5.	d 5	d	3

If White does not occupy this point, Black goes there and secures the second corner with the strongest possible base formation. On page 114 it was pointed out in connection with the position in the lower right corner of Diagram 33 that whoever plays the second stone in the corner will obtain an advantage, and that therefore it was not advisable to leave the approach from the intersection of the fifth and fourth lines unanswered. In approaching the corner from this point before the opponent had occupied the intersection of the third and fourth lines Karigane almost forces Honinbo to take up an unfavourable position.

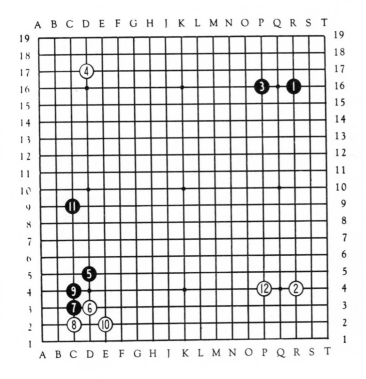

DIAGRAM 45

7. c 3	c 2
9. c 4	e 2
11. c 9	p 4

White takes up a high position in this corner because his position is low in the neighbouring corner.

Since this is the point toward which normal extension tends from Black's upper right base as well as from White's lower right, the advantage is here on White's side. The reason why Black did not occupy this point was no doubt that he did not want to permit White to form a base securing the upper left corner.

15. g 17   e 16

This is the play most frequently employed to develop a stone from the intersection of the third and fourth lines. The position of the two White stones prepares placing a man between the Black stones on c9 and c15 as well as between stone g17 and the upper right corner. Black strengthens his stone c15 because it is closer to the two White stones and therefore more in need of protection than g17.

17. d 13   c 16

With this and the next move White secures the corner which Black would otherwise invade with b17, sandwiching the White men.

19. d 15   b 16

Without this move Black would still have a chance to attack the corner with c18, threatening to connect with his man on g17 via e 18 or with his man on c15 via b16. Black has now re-gained Sente and can use it either for an invasion of the territory on the lower edge of the board or for an attack against White's outpost on the right side.

21. r 12   l 17

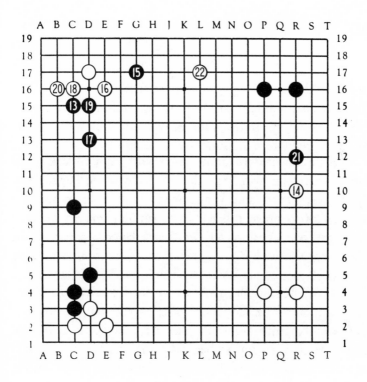

DIAGRAM 46

This is the best spot on the upper edge. If White had played m17, Black would have answered k17, which is the logical extension from g17, and White would find himself sandwiched between two strong positions. With k17 White would have exerted stronger pressure against g17, but Black would have been able to extend to m17, gaining control over a very large territory in the corner. Black need not reply to l 17, because g17 is not yet very strongly threatened. He therefore continues his attack on the right side.

$$23. \text{ r } 8 \qquad\qquad \text{q } 12$$

This threatens the invasion r13 into Black's prospective territory on the upper right and must therefore be answered. The move is a subtle preparation for the following five plays with which White restricts the activity of Black's outpost on the lower right to a minimum and retains Sente.

If White attacked r8 immediately with 24.p9, Black could connect his man with r12 through 25.q10, q9; 27.r9, q11; 29.s10, r11; 31.s11, and White would still have to make a move so as to prevent Black from running out at p10 and splitting White's position in two. Black could accomplish the connection also with 25.s10, s11; 27.r11, s9; 29.q10, r9; 31.q9, t10*; 33.p8, both lines obviously being good for Black.

With a White stone at q12, however, these connections would not work out favorably for Black: 25.r13, p9; 27.q10, q9; 29.r9 would permit White to play r11, and Black could not cut White off with 31.q11 because of 32.p11. Or: 27.s10, s11; 29.r11, s9; 31.q10, r9; 33.q9, q8, and Black must guard against the Sh'cho threatened with q11, so that his man on r8 is cut off and White's territory on the lower left is kept unimpaired.

A White man on q11 would actually produce a Sh'cho although the Black chain apparently saves itself through connection with g17. However, with the aid of his man on l17, White can force the fleeing men down one line as they reach k16 and catch them.

$$25. \quad \text{ r } 13 \qquad\qquad \text{p } 9$$
$$27. \quad \text{ p } 7 \qquad\qquad \text{q } 7$$

Again an example of a cut following a "Knight's move." If

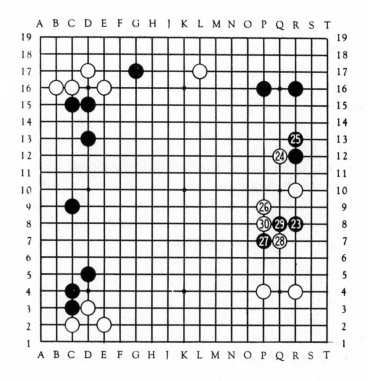

DIAGRAM 47

Black had recognized White's deep plan to form a vertical wall on the right and to develop his position in the lower left then with e5, walling off a territory of tremendous size on the lower side of the board, he might have continued now with 29.q6, q8; 31.r5, q4; 33.o6, r7; 35.s5, m3; 37.h3.

29. q 8   p 8

31.	q	6	o	7
33.	r	7*	o	6

The wall is now erected. Black must spend one more move on the little group just formed in order to connect it with his position on the upper right so that he need not worry about Me, and that gives White the tempo he needs to start on the other wall on the left.

35.	s	10	e	5

It might be mentioned in passing that s9 would not effectively cut the two Black groups, because the consequence would be 37.r9,s11; 39. q10, r11; 41. t10, s8; 43.q11, s12; 45. s13, and the White group has only one Me. If instead of s8 White plays q11, Black plays s8 and obtains two Me.

37.	e	6	f	5

Black was, of course, aware of the fact that with e6 he provokes a strengthening of White's group with f5, which makes it extremely dangerous to attempt the formation of a position near the lower edge of the board, from where Black cannot hope to communicate with the centre, but must rely upon being able to form two Me. But if Black had placed a man on the lower side of the board right away, let us say at k3 or k4, White could have played e6 with the threat to cut into the territory at the left, at the same time isolating still more the intended base of Black near the lower edge. With e6 Black strengthens his influence on the left side tremendously, so that he may hope to find sufficient compensation there in case he loses his men with which he plans to invade the White territory below.

39.	f3		d	4

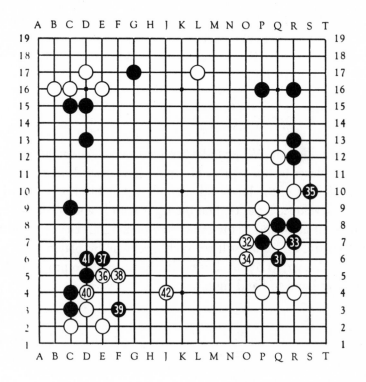

DIAGRAM 48

This forces Black to protect himself against the cut at c5 first, which threatens to win the men at c3 and c4.

41. d 6   i 4

Preventing the cut at e4, which would now be answered with g3. The way Karigane boldly develops a position and finally cuts e4 all the same is most ingenious; it took a Honinbo to refute his plan. Attack and defense, in the following struggle, which lasts about one hundred moves, are fairly easily understood. It soon becomes evident that Black cannot form two Me and can live only if he succeeds in breaking part of the chain which strangles him.

43.	k3		i	3
45.	i	2	k	4

With this move White indicates that he wants to catch all men Black places in this region. He could have played h2, securing the left half of the lower side definitely, but Black would then have developed a position on the right with l2 and l5, threatening a cut at o5 and at the same time making an escape toward the centre. He could still try such a scheme by playing 47.l 3, h2; 49. k1, g3; 51.o3 etc., but evidently he wants to provoke the ensuing hand to hand fight.

47.	k	2	l	3
49.	l	2	m	3
51.	m	2	n	2
53.	h	3		

At this point the game was adjourned. In the forenoon of the second day only three moves were made in two hours, so difficult was the decision for Black, whether to play merely for the safety of his persecuted group or for a counter-attack by cutting at e4.

53.	. . .		h	4
55.	g	4	g	5
57.	n	3	o	2
59.	f	2	h	2

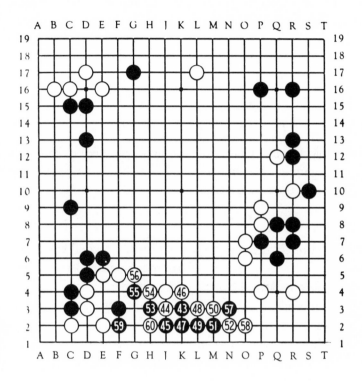

DIAGRAM 49

Black could now save his men by producing a Ko with g2,
for he has more threats than White. Three threats would arise
from a cut at l 4 and two more from an attack on n2 and o2 by
o3. Furthermore two threats were available against White's position in the upper left corner, at c18 and e18. But White would
surely have obtained a good many points when finally Black

captured the man on h2 without answering what threat White may have made on the previous move. And so Black decides to risk the life of his whole group against the chance to capture a part of the surrounding chain by cuts at l 4 and h5, which, if successful, would cut White's territory down to very little and ensure Black's victory.

| 61. | g | 3 | f | 1 |
| 63. | g | 1 | m | 1 |

To protect f1 by e1 is not only unnecessary, because f1 would not be a genuine Me, but it would be a bad blunder, because Black would then secure two eyes with h1.

| 65. | h | 1 | l | 1 |

This definitely destroys the possibility of a second eye. Black cannot play k1 as i1 would kill six men. He deliberated three hours before making his next move, obvious as it seems to us ordinary mortals that the cut at e4 was his only chance either to win by the counter-attack on the lower left corner or at least to make White add a number of stones on the lower edge to kill the Black men and to utilize that time to enlarge his influence on the centre from the left wing.

| 67. | e | 4 | b | 2 |
| 69. | g | 2* | k | 1 |

The reader might wonder why Black did not now continue with 71.e3, d2; 73.b3. This apparently would have given him the opportunity to save the larger part of his army and capture White's corner group by sacrificing his five men around k2. For example: 74.a3; 75.b5, n1; 77.e1*, i1; 79.d1, h2*5; 81.b1!, f4; 83.i2*, k2; 85.c1, winning. Or: 76.e1: 77.a2, a1*; 79.c1, n1; 81.b1!, d1*2; 83.b1, c1*; 85.a4, i1; 85.a2, again winning. How-

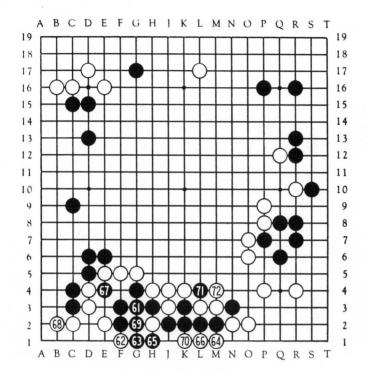

DIAGRAM 50

ever, the combination has a flaw. White does not capture at
a1 on his 78th move. Instead, he immediately proceeds with
n1, and only after 79.b1, i1; 81.c1, he captures in the corner.
Black then has no Ko threat large enough to keep White
from playing f4, and Black's men die.

71. l 4   m 4

73.	l	5		k	5
75.	o	3		p	2

Not p3, because i1 followed by p2 would win the White men on the edge.

77.	n	1		o	1*

The sacrifice of this man gives Black the opportunity for a Ko threat by i1 and p3.

79.	h	5		h	6
81.	k	6		i	5*
83.	i	6		h	5

When we look at the position now, we begin to realize that the three hours which Black pondered over his 67th move were probably not spent in vain. He has succeeded in turning upon his opponent and has forced him to flee. It is true, he can save his trapped men only if his opponent's flight is unsuccessful, but even then his position has much improved because he has shut off the oppressing White chain from the centre, gaining a strong influence there himself. He must now pause to make a defensive move again, to avoid White's cutting at l 6, but in doing so he threatens the four White men around m3, which must be defended in order not to provide an avenue of escape for the large Black chain at the lower edge.

85.	l	6		n	1

This threatens i1 and e3 so that Black cannot play n5 at this time.

87.	i	1		n	4
89.	h	7		g	7
91.	f	6		h	8

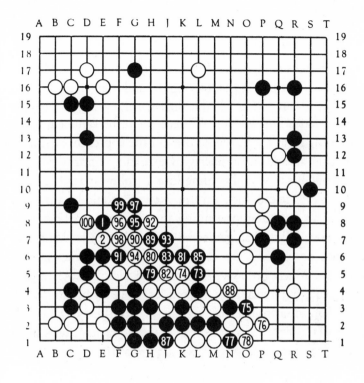

DIAGRAM 51

93.	i	7	g	6
95.	g	8	f	8
97.	g	9	f	7
99.	f	9	d	8
101.	e	8	e	7

The obvious continuation 103.e9, d7 would leave White with

[161]

three breathing-spaces in addition to f4, while the more subtle play which Black chooses permits him only two, apart from adding a breathing-space to the men around d6.

103. d 7   e 9*

Let us analyze whether Black could not have saved himself here by first playing e3, forcing d2, and then continuing, as he does, with e10. After c8; 109. d9, e8; 111. c7, b8; 113. b7, the situation looks hopeless for White, because he cannot play e1, threatening f4, as 115.b9 would prevent the approach. He might try to gain an additional liberty by extending northward with 114.b9, but Black would confine him as follows: 115.b10, b11; 117.c11, a10; 119.c10, b12; 121.b13. Now e1 would be answered with 123.a8, definitely preventing the approach on f4.

However, White has gained so many liberties by his extension that he can win by capturing the Black group on the lower left. A neat little sacrifice turns the trick: 122.c5!; 123.b5, b4: 125.c6*, b3; 127.a7, a5; 129.c12, c5*^{2}; (Playing a6 instead would be a disastrous error, because of 131.a12, c5*^{2}; 133.c4*, c3; 135.a11*^{2}, c5*; 137.a4!, a3*; 139.c4*, a4; 141.a9*, winning.) 131.c4*, c3; 133.a12, c5*; 135.b6, a4; 137.a11*^{2}, c4, etc.

105. e 10   e 3

Not c8 because of 107. d9, e8; 109. e3, d2; 111.b8, c7; 113. b6, and the White army falls.

107. d 9   f 4*
109. e 1*   d 2

He cannot play d1, because e8* would win immediately.

111. b 3   c 8

White deliberated over an hour and a half before making this

[162]

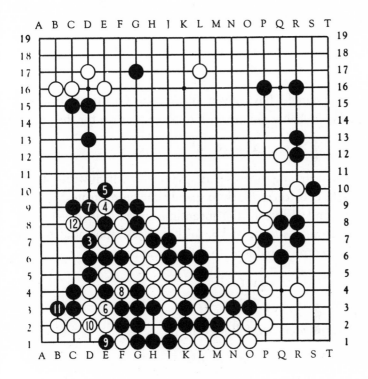

DIAGRAM 52

move! He probably considered carefully all Ko threats which Black has at his disposal and came to the conclusion that he had time to kill the Black army at the lower edge in spite of answering all threats.

113. e 8*   e 4

This threatens to cut at c5. In view of the Ko, Black should probably have now replied c5 and not b5, which allows another threat at c5.

115.	b	5	e	9*
117.	n	5	o	4

117.o4 would have given Black two Ko threats instead of one. He probably did not wish to give up a man for the purpose.

119.	e	8*	c	5

This surprising move is perhaps the play which wins the game for White. It forces Black to spend time on securing Me for his group, and White in the meantime succeeds in developing a chain from his stone at h8, so that Black's potential territory in the centre is reduced to insignificant size.

121.	b	8	e	9*
123.	c	7	e	8

This threatens b7, followed by b9.

125.	c	6*	b	9

Now Black cannot very well play b7, guarding his group on the lower left solidly and thereby threatening again an attack against the White men in the lower left corner by d1 and e2, for White would reply d10, and after 129. c10, d11; 131. c11, d12, Black must protect himself against the Sh'cho attack threatened by a cut at f11 and thus permit White to play c12, whereupon the Black men at d13, d15, and c15 are isolated and will be badly pressed by e13 after he has guarded the threat b10.

127.	b	10	f	10
129.	e	11	h	9

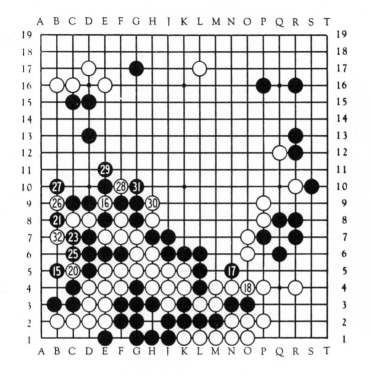

DIAGRAM 53

131. g 10   b 7

This and the following three moves of White constitute an
ingenious manœuvre to prevent Black from attacking with a2,
without losing Sente. If Black is permitted to play a2, d1; b1, a
Ko comes about which Black could utilize to capture the White
men on h8 and h9 by playing h10 and i9, resulting in permanent

strength of the chain extending from l 4 to g10, so that a great deal of centre territory is likely to fall to Black. No doubt White had all these contingencies in mind when he played 120.c5.

| 133. | a 9* | b 6 |
| 135. | c 5 | a 4 |

Now that a2 is prevented, since a3 would be the answer, Black must look out for his group in the centre.

| 137. | k 9 | a 3 |

Threatening a5.

| 139. | a 7 | g 11 |

A sacrifice to help develop the men at h8 and h9 with threats against the Black group around g10.

141.	h 10	i 10
143.	h 11	i 9
145.	h 12	i 12
147.	l 10	h 13
149.	g 12	i 11
151.	l 12	l 13
153.	m 12	m 9

This threatens to cut at k8 and at the same time prevents Black from cutting at o8. White has emerged with a decided positional advantage, for the Black group in the centre must now fight for its life, while the White centre chain establishes connection with l 17 and threatens to gain territory in the upper left centre as well as to extend toward the upper right corner.

155.	l 9	m 7
157.	l 7	g 13
159.	f 12	k 13

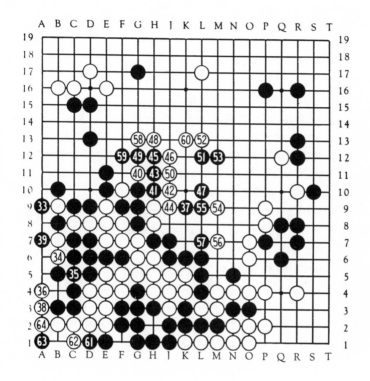

DIAGRAM 54

Black now makes a last attempt to throw the lower left corner into Ko because he hopes to profit by Ko threats which White will not be able to answer without endangering the life of his large army in the lower left quarter of the board.

161. d 1   c 1
163. a 1   a 2

[167]

White must answer or Black plays a2, b1*2; 167.a2, and White cannot play a1*, as 169.a2 would capture his whole army. He would therefore have to play 169.f1*2, e1*, after which the Ko situation would be acute, Black needing only three moves, a5, a6, and b4, to attack the White group, while White also requires three moves, a1*, a2, and d1, to approach the Black army.

In surveying the position on the whole board we find that White has about fifty points along the lower edge, including the nineteen men which he will capture there, while Black has about thirty points on the right side and in the upper right corner and about twenty points on the upper left side.

White has in addition ten or twelve points in the upper left corner and he threatens to secure another ten points, approximately, in the upper centre, beginning possibly with g16.

The only chance which Black has to secure additional territory is by extension from the upper right corner toward l 17. His own chain in the centre is still subject to attack, and so is White's chain on that part of the board. Black therefore chooses a move which keeps White's centre chain from connecting with the group in the upper left, at the same time invading the territory in the upper centre to which White would otherwise lay claim.

165. f 15   n 14

White's move threatens Black's centre chain and prepares connection with l 17.

167.	m 10	q 13
169.	n 13	o 13
171.	o 14	m 13
173.	n 12	n 15

The weakness of Black's centre chain, which has forced him to make safeguarding moves while White was able to use his

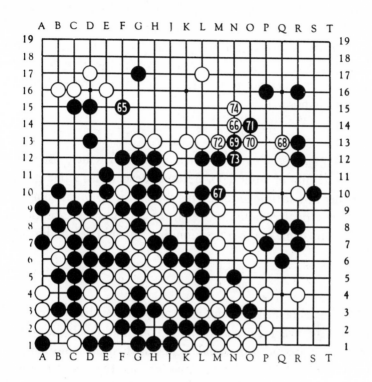

DIAGRAM 55

oppressing stones at the same time for formation of additional
territory, is really what loses the game in the end for Black.
White now succeeds in developing his stone 1 17 into a position
by extending to o17, as Black must lose a move to wall off his
right wing against an invasion which White could start with
o15, connecting his two groups in the left and right centre. As

[169]

long as Black keeps these two armies separated, they remain at least attackable, though they can easily save themselves. But the mere fact that they remain subject to attack is an advantage, for Ko threats as well as for economical play by Black, who still faces a fight in the upper left centre, where his stone g17 must be saved in order not to let the surrounding territory fall into White's hands.

175.   o 15   o 17

The great problem for Black is now whether, after this strengthening of stone l 17, he must develop his stone g17 or whether he has time to fortify his corner with p17. He took two and three quarter hours to weigh the attacking possibilities of White and came to the conclusion that he could defend himself.

177.   p 17   o 16
179.   p 15   m 8

White deliberated an hour and three quarters before deciding upon this move. He probably figured out that the attack against the region around g17 would yield less than he could gain by keeping the Black centre chain under the necessity of forming Me and utilizing the time Black must take for defence to wall off the group in the right centre, which Black might otherwise cut into from q10.

181.   o 12   s 11
183.   r 11   q 10
185.   s 9   q 11

White has maintained Sente, for Black must meet the threat r14. He could do so with q14, but then White would have two or three Ko threats at his disposal by cutting at r14.

187.   r 14   f 16

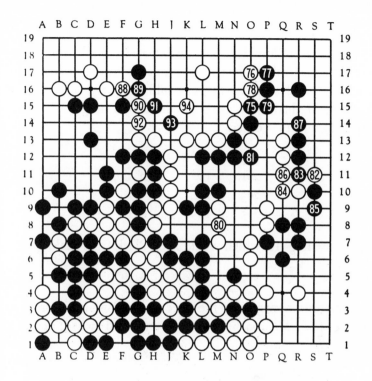

DIAGRAM 56

At last the long-expected attack against g17.

189.	g 16	g 15
191.	h 15	g 14
193.	i 14	k 15

This prevents i13, as i15 would follow, and at the same time it eats into the space Black would like to use to form Me.

[171]

195.	k 18	l 18
197.	e 18	d 18

White had to lose this move, as otherwise Black would play c18 with an attack on the corner, the consequences of which are almost beyond analysis. Black would not have succeeded in forming Me had it not been for the tempo he gained by the threat against the corner.

199.	i 15	i 13
201.	i 17	h 18
203.	g 18	i 16
205.	k 16	k 17

Threatening i18, which would keep Black from making Me.

207.	i 18	l 16*

Black must now give up the three men around i15 in order to be sure of two Me. 209. h16 would be answered by h19; 211. g19, e19.

209.	h 19	p 18
211.	q 18	f 1*2

Now that fight about all major territories has reached an end, the time has come to attend to the Ko in the lower left corner, which would decide the life or death of the White army surrounding the Black group on the lower edge as soon as Black has made the three moves a6, a5, and b4.

213.	e 1*	d 1

Here is the Ko. Black now first removes White's man on o13, because if he permitted his connection to q13 he would have to

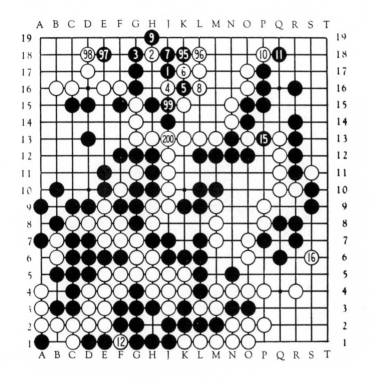

DIAGRAM 57

lose time substantiating his Me at k7 and l 11 under Ko threats of White.

215.   p 13*   s 6

This end-game move is worth about eight points as against the position which would arise if Black had time to play s5.

217.	a	6*2	f	1*
219.	b	15	e	15

If White permitted Black to connect at e15, the Black territory on the upper left side would increase considerably and White would have to make a move forming Me in the corner. Since White has several Ko threats at his disposal, he can afford to answer here instead of capturing at h2.

221.	e	1*	l	8

This threat is worth about twenty-five points, twice the number of the Black men which are threatened to be cut off and the adjoining points which are neutral at this moment.

223.	k	8	f	1*
225.	f	14	f	13
227.	e	14	b	18
229.	e	1*	e	13
231.	d	14	f	1*
233.	n	16	h	2*14

White does not continue the Ko, but captures the Black group and gives up whatever Black's last Ko threat involved, because it is evident that Black has more threats at his disposal; and since White has figured out that he wins in spite of the 15 points which he yields by not answering Black's last threat, there is no object in risking further complications which might arise from Black's continuing m16 when it is his turn next to make a Ko threat.

235.	n	17	e	12

The end-game stage has been reached. White, having Sente, almost makes up for the fifteen points lost on the upper right by

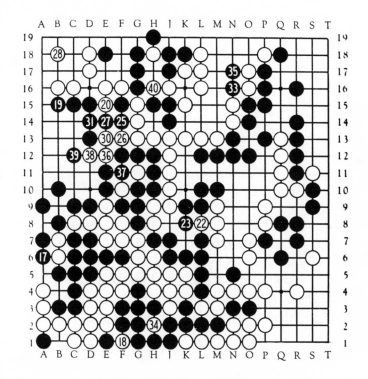

DIAGRAM 58

his last move, which, in connection with the next move, results in a loss of about seven or eight points for Black, and by h16, which is worth seven points.

237. f 11*2   d 12
239. c 12   h 16

241.	h 17*	k 16
243.	m 15	m 14
245.	m 16	l 15

Without this move the White centre chain lacks space for two eyes.

247.	s 7	s 5
249.	n 9	p 6
251.	n 6	o 10
253.	n 10	o 8

At this point Karigane resigned the game because he had only ten minutes left in which to finish the game, and though only a few end games have to be played out, the decision in which order to play them would require more time, and the final result would be White's victory in any case.

Only two points are at stake at most of the spots where the frontiers have not yet been completely drawn. At o11 and q5, perhaps three. But in the majority of these end games White retains Sente and therefore he gains a few more points. The Diagram shows one possible version of the finish. Another version might run thus:

255.	q 14	d 11
257.	c 11	a 15
259.	a 14	a 16
261.	b 14	q 5
263.	o 5	p 5
265.	o 11	e 17
267.	f 18	n 18
269.	o 18*2	m 18
271.	k 11	o 19
273.	p 19*	n 19

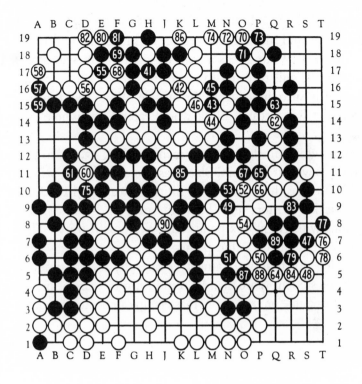

DIAGRAM 59

Now no moves are left which would gain a point for one player or the other. The game is over, and the Dame points remain to be filled in. In the course of filling in these Dame stones Black will find himself attacked on k7 so that he will have to fill this spot. White needs a man on k14 to form two Me, because Black will threaten k14 after the White centre chain is completely surrounded from the outside. White could then not connect at l 14, because Black would capture the whole group with h 14.

After removing the captured men from a1, n3, o3, h15, i15, and i14 as well as from s11, Black has a total of twenty prisoners and White has thirty-one. After filling the captured Black men into Black's territory and the White men into White's, Black remains with twenty-six points and White with thirty. Therefore White wins with four points.

Playing this beautiful game over carefully several times will teach the student more than he could learn in years of practice. No better guide on the way to mastership can be imagined.

« 4 »
ADVANCED STRATEGY

In the game of Go, as in Chess, the player who makes the first move has the advantage that he can occupy points of strategic importance ahead of his opponent, with the result that the second player has to struggle for equality throughout the opening phase of the contest. There is, however, a fundamental difference between the two games in the type of strategy which is advisable for the second player. In Chess, he is very likely to get into trouble if he makes an early attempt at seizing the initiative instead of confining himself to defensive play until he has completed his development. In Go, the second player must play aggressively almost from the very start, or he will emerge from the opening with a positional disadvantage very difficult to overcome — provided, of course, his opponent is approximately his equal in strength.

Aggressive and defensive play

Aggressive play does not necessarily imply early hand-to-hand fighting, though it does mean confronting the enemy closely enough to lay the basis for such a fight, rather than merely striving for territorial expansion without actual invasion of the opponent's grounds.

In the game discussed in detail in the preceding chapter, White might have answered Black's first move with 2.p17, as illustrated in Diagram 60, thereby signifying his intention to obtain a share of the territory in this corner at the first opportune moment. A very good reply for Black would be 3.e16, inviting White to contest this corner with c16, which he would counter with 5.l17. The stones e16 and l17 would serve as outposts for a sizable prospective territory along the upper edge and threaten squeeze plays against White's man on p17 as well as against the one on c16.

Even if White does not play c16 but instead occupies a point in one of the lower corners, c5, for example, Black's 5.l17 would be a strong move, because of the threat 7.q17, p16; 9.q14, encircling the White men. Their flight toward the left would entail an extension from l17 on the part of Black which would greatly increase his potential territory along the upper edge.

There are many ways in which White can defend himself against this threat. He can play r17, for example, or p14, or q14 as assumed in the Diagram. The most natural continuation for Black in this case is 7.p16, severing the communication between the two White stones. After the reply 8.o16, the sequence 9.p15, q17; 11.r15, r17; 13.r11 might ensue, with the result that White has seized the valuable corner territory which would otherwise have fallen to Black. In exchange, however, Black has consolidated a position on the upper right side. While this position is smaller than White's corner territory, Black's man on l17 will surely be helpful in securing additional territory in conjunction with the one on e16. White's man on q14, on the other hand, has practically no further significance, and the situation remains in Black's favor.

White will, of course, place his next stone in the remaining vacant corner. Instead of choosing q4, as shown in the Diagram, he could occupy p4; but q3 or r4 would be disadvantageous. In reply to q3 Black would play 15.r5, greatly increasing his

[180]

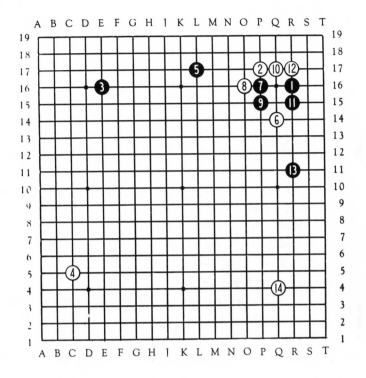

DIAGRAM 60

influence along the right side; and in reply to r4 he would continue with 15.p3, threatening a squeeze play such as 17.q5, r5; 19.q6, which would drive White toward the strong Black position on the upper right and at the same time prepare a wide extension along the lower edge.

For his fifteenth move Black has many alternatives to choose from. Most plausible seems c16, securing the upper left corner, or an invasion of the lower side prepared by pressure against White's man in the lower left corner. This man could be confronted either from d3 or, as illustrated in the Diagram, from e4.

After 15.e4, d3; 17.e3, White could defend the corner with d4 as well as with the diagrammed move d2. Black's reply to d4 would be 19.e5, and White would ensure communication with the centre with 20.d6, which would also make an invasion of the left side more difficult for Black. 18.d2 requires the answer 19.l3 (compare page 69); otherwise White would squeeze with l4, at the same time securing a very large space on the lower right.

Next, White will establish a foothold in the upper left, to reduce as much as possible Black's large potential territory in that region. Ordinarily White would start the invasion with 20.c16 (see move 6 in the Honinbo-Karigane game). But in view of the Black outpost on l17 White avoids the standard sequence 21.c17, b17; 23.d17, b15, which would leave Black with considerably more space than he can secure after the diagrammed move 20.c17. Black cannot shut White in with 21.c15, because d16; 23.d15, e17 would follow. Then, after 25.f17, f18 Black must guard against f16, enabling White to push on with g18. This sequence would cost Black a great many points. The defense shown in the Diagram,. 21.d17, c16; 23.e14, c13; is therefore much preferable. Black not only emerges with more territory but besides retains Sente, which he can use very effectively for an attack against the White position in the upper right: 25.o15, n16; 27.n18 (threatening the cut at o17), o18; 29.n17, o17; 31.l15. This completes the bottling-up operation and at the same time solidifies the right boundary of Black's large territory in a manner which will

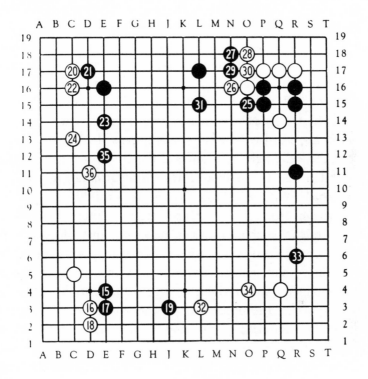

DIAGRAM 61

make invasion very difficult. As a matter of fact, as soon as important Ko threats become available to Black, he could start a dangerous attack on the whole White position in the upper right with s17, answering the defense s18 with t18. Then s16 and t16 would produce a Ko.

Winding up the opening phase, White will add to his territory by an extension from q4. 32.l3 is better suited for this purpose than r9, because Black's position on the lower edge is weaker than that on the upper right side. 33.r6 and 34.o4 will be the natural continuations, when corners and side positions are sufficiently clearly staked off to begin middle game operations. Black has a powerful move at his disposal in 35.e12. After this, an invasion of his enormous territory in the upper half of the board will be practically impossible. The move also strengthens the fighting chances of the three Black men on the lower left and furthermore threatens an invasion of the left side which White will probably have to ward off with 36.d11.

A rough estimate of the prospective territory Black and White might be able to consolidate reveals that Black is very likely some twenty points ahead. White may wind up with about fifty points on the left, twenty-five on the lower right, and ten in the upper right, or a total of eighty-five. Black's huge space in the upper half of the board alone embraces almost one hundred points, and he will have another few points left in his position near the lower edge.

The lower half of the board, of course, is not yet clarified to a degree which would make an evaluation possible. The three Black men on the left are still vulnerable, and the two on the right are more so. In pressing against these weak men White is bound to gain quite a little space.

Attack and defense of corner positions The manner in which more or less widely spaced stones which stake off territory of the enemy are best attacked or separated is one of the problems which the inexperienced player has a hard time in solving. The following examples deal with a few typical positions which are apt to arise in handicap games. In Diagram 62 Black, on the move, has the choice of defending his corner with either f4 or d6. As a

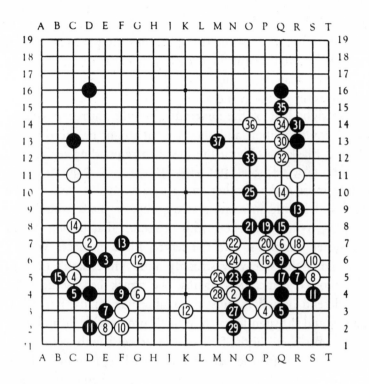

DIAGRAM 62

matter of general principle it would appear preferable to
choose 1.f4, because the attack on c6 would drive White's man
toward his outpost on c11, with the likelihood that White
will form a sizable safe position between lines 6 and 11.
Analysis shows that this judgment is indeed correct. The
course of the Joseki beginning with 1.d6 would be: d7; 3.e6,

c5; 5.c4, g4; 7.e3, e2; 9.f4, f2; 11.d2, g6; 13.f7, c8. White has established connection between his men on c6 and c11, and he has maintained Sente, for Black must still make a move to defend himself against the threat c2, for example 15.b5. Otherwise White would steal the corner with 16.c2; 17.d1, c3; 19.d3, b4. With a man on b5, however, Black would not have to fear this invasion of the corner.

The right half of the Diagram gives the mirror picture of the opening position and shows what might be the development if Black starts with the move corresponding to f4.

After 1.o4, n4; 3.o5, p3; 5.q3, q7; 7.r5, s5; 9.q6, s6; 11.s4, White must make another move to develop his men on the third and fourth lines into a safe group, or Black would play 13.l4, n5; 15.n6, m5; 17.o6, with the result that having pulled his corner group out into the centre, Black menaces White's men along the side very strongly and White hasn't time to take protective measures against the attack because he must first defend himself against the manoeuvre 19.m3, n3; 21.k3. This would threaten to catch White's group with l6, and after White goes there himself Black can proceed with 23.r9, or he can extend toward the left on the third line, forming a large territory and still keeping White's group hanging in the air. 23.r9, q10; 25.q8, p6; 27.q5, r7; 29.p8, p7; 31.o8, s9; 33.s10, s8; 35.r10, t7 would let the White group live but conquer a tremendous amount of territory in the upper quadrant so that this line would not be playable at all. Thus White would do best to play 12.k3, as shown in the Diagram.

Again Black will invade White's territory with 13.r9 and answer q10 with 15.q8, p6; 17.q5, r7; 19.p8, p7; 21.o8. But White can now save both halves of his group which Black has cut in two. With 22.n7 White threatens to encircle Black's corner group with n5, which would at the same time connect

[186]

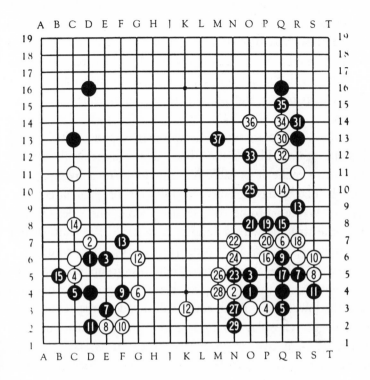

DIAGRAM 62

all White's stones in the lower quadrant and also permit White to play o10, with strong pressure on Black's four stones on lines 8 and 9. Black counters both threats with 23.n5. Now he threatens in turn to cut off White's army with 25.o7, o6; 27.n6 without being endangered himself, so that White must defend with 24.n6. This gives Black time for 25.o10, which gets his four men out of danger and prepares a killing assault on White's men at r11 and q10. Their death would leave Black in possession of about fifty points in the upper quadrant and White must therefore try to save them at all cost. He maintains Sente through 26.m5, which revives the old threat s3. Black eliminates this threat with 27.n3, m4; 29.n2, winning the two White men on o3 and p3, a gain which is worth about ten points.

White's best plan would now be to expand with 30.q13. Threats against Black's men both in the upper right and in the centre make it possible for him to form a living group, though Black, having succeeded in his original attempt to destroy White's prospective territory along the side, emerges from the struggle with a definite advantage. The continuation might be: 31.r14, q12; 33.o12, q14; 35.q15, o14; 37.m13.

Even if White should strengthen his group on the right side, with 12.o7 threatening n5, before safeguarding his men near the lower edge, Black could still invade the space between r6 and r11. The play might run like this (see Diagram 63): 13.n6, l3; 15.r9, q10; 17.q8, p6; 19.q5, r7; 21.p8, o8; 23.p9, p7; 25.o9, n9; 27.p11. Again White's territory has been destroyed.

Invasions It is most desirable to place the invading stones so that they cannot be capped from the outside, so that they can escape into the centre if it turns out that they cannot capture one of the parts of the opponent's group which they have severed. Thus, in our example, if after 1.c9 (left half of Diagram 63) d10, Black played 3.d9, allowing e9, he would be taking a dangerous chance. Indeed, after 5.d8, e6; 7.d5, e7; 9.e8, f8; 11.f9, e10; 13.f7, g8; 15.c7, b7; 17.c8, f6; 19.b10, White wins the Black group through 20.c10, as 21.b9, b11 leaves Black with only three liberties against four of White.

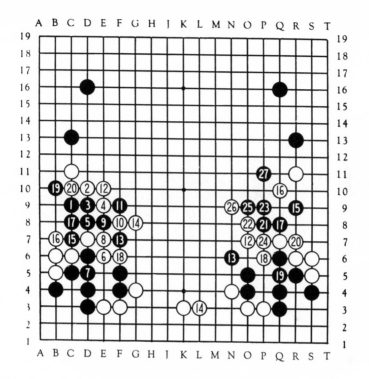

DIAGRAM 63

The variations analyzed in the discussion of this opening will furnish an inkling of the subtle considerations often required for the proper choice of a move even at the initial stage of the game. The student should note that the invasion at r11 was justified only because it could be expected to result in a squeeze effect with the aid of the stones at r13 and q16.

The wider the extension which a player has made from a stone to stake off territory, the more vulnerable he becomes, of course, to invasion threats. The widest extension ever undertaken is a skip of five points, as shown in Diagram 64, and such a jump is feasible only when the extending stone is not confronting more than one man. Preferably the opponent should not yet be established at all in the neighborhood of the extending stone, as in the case here illustrated. If it were Black's move, he could make sure of conquering a great deal of space by the sequence 1.q5, r5; 3.q6, r7; 5.q7, r8; 7.q8, q9; 9.p9. That is why White is compelled to answer the extension i3 by placing a man on either q5 or q6, either of these two moves being preferable to a mere extension on line r.

In reply to White's 1.q5 Black must guard against an invasion at l3 with 2.n4. If White played 1.q6, Black should guard with 2.m4, which would protect his territory even if White continued with 3.o6, while he would have to defend himself with either m4 or l4, if in reply to q6 he had extended only as far as n4.

Let us see what White's invasion would lead to in case Black fails to guard against it. As indicated in the Diagram, White would follow up 1.q5 with 3.l3. Black would then first separate the invader from his base in the corner through p5, and play would continue with 5.p6, o5; 7.q3, q2; 9.r2. Now Black would try to surround the intruder at l3 beginning with 10.k4; but White escapes with 11.m5. Black cannot cut with l4; 13.m4, m3, because 15.n3, m2; 17.n2, l2; 19.o3 would connect White's groups via p2 or p4, and destroy Black's territory. For example: 20.o2; 21.p4, p2; 23.o4, n1; 25.o6, etc.

It is interesting to note that if Black originally had extended only one point less, to k3 instead of l3, White would not threaten the invasion m3 when playing q5, because after the

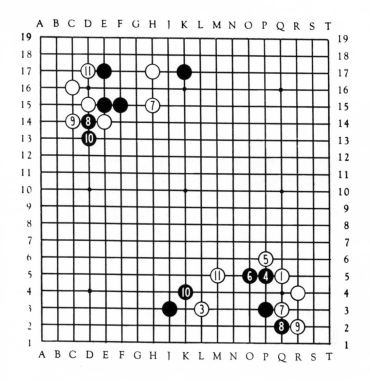

DIAGRAM 64

same first nine moves which are shown in the Diagram, when Black continues with 10.l4, White cannot escape capture. 11.n5 would be met with n4; 13.m4, m5; 15.n6, n3, etc. The best White could do would probably be to adopt the procedure illustrated in the upper left of the Diagram, where the 7th move is used to come out into the centre. In reply to the cut

8.d14 he should then continue with 9.c14 and 11.d17, securing his corner territory. If he tried, instead, to capture Black through 9.d13, he would fail because c14; 11.c13, b15 would follow and after White guards his corner with 13.b16, Black gets away with b13. White cannot stop him with 15.b12, as e13; 17.f14, e12 would threaten c12 as well as g14, catching the two men on line 14 through Sh'cho.

Diagram 65 shows an example of an invasion made for the sole purpose of having the enemy lose time with moves which kill the invader, while the invader utilizes that time to consolidate a larger amount of space than that represented by the invaded territory.

Black, on the move, would like to play 1.k3 without giving White the opportunity to attack the corner with 2.f3. He accomplishes this by first invading White's territory with 1.c7. The natural reaction to this is 2.e5, preventing attempts of connecting c7 with d3, and at the same time threatening an invasion at l3. Black would counter with 3.f4, and after White makes sure of capturing c7 by placing a man on d8, the continuation 5.c4, b5; 7.f5 (threatening d6), d7; 9.l3 would lay claim to a very large number of points.

If White, to prevent this, played 4.l3, Black would, of course, run out to the centre with 5.e7 and meet the reply 6.f5 with 7.g4. This would force White to develop a safe group around l3 without delay, and Black could keep White's men on line c from connecting with 9.b7.

In the position shown in the upper half of the Diagram, White's first impulse would be to play 1.l17, exerting a squeeze on p17 and preparing to stake off a large territory with 3.d15. However, this would be the wrong sequence of moves. Black would counter with 2.e16; 3.e17, f16; 5.g17, g16; 7.h17 and then make a wide extension downward on line c. White should start with 1.d15, and when, after d14; 3.e15, c16; 5.c17 Black

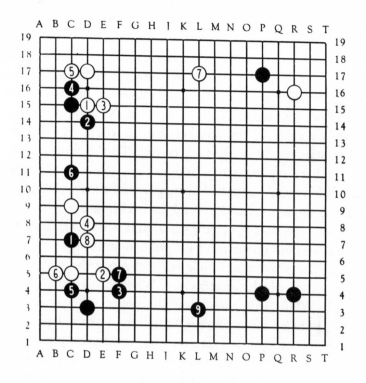

DIAGRAM 65

defends with 6.c11, White accomplishes his purpose with 7l.17.

Black cannot very well play 6.l17 instead of c11, because White would immediately attack the group around c15 with 7.d12, threatening e14, and after 8.e14; 9.f14, e13; 11.c13, c14 Black would remain with a hanging chain, while White, extending downward on line c, can form a position worth many points.

An important strategic procedure to understand is the proper method of attack against a corner staked off with two men on the fourth line from the edge as illustrated in Diagram 66.

If the attacking player has a stone on either side of the corner in question, as in the upper right of the Diagram, while the defending player has not yet established himself on the sides, the direct approach 1.r15 to the lower of the two defending stones is in order. This will result in a division of territory more favorable to the attacker than he could have reached when starting with either r13 or n17. To the former, Black would have replied 2.m17, and to the latter 2.r12. In either case White would have had to answer with a move strengthening the single man which Black had confronted.

After 1.r15, q15; 3.r14, s16; 5.q14, p14; 7.p13, o14; 9.o13, n14 White has built up a respectable position on the right side and he can also seize considerable territory along the upper edge with 11.n17, which threatens q17. When Black defends with 12.o18, White will consolidate his upper left corner with 13.f16, to avoid an attack beginning with 14.h17. This move, in conjunction with the man on n14, would exert pressure on the position k17-n17 and compel White to strengthen it: Besides, Black would be developing a base from which to invade the corner.

If a black stone were on r10 instead of the white one, the manoeuvre described above would be altogether uncalled for, as it would provoke the building of a huge area on the upper right edge by Black. The proper method of approaching Black would be 1.r13, instead. This would leave open the possibility of a later invasion at m17.

The direct assault with 1.r15 would be doubly dubious if White had no stone on k17 and were not backed up by a stone on r9 or r10 either. After the first ten moves shown in Diagram

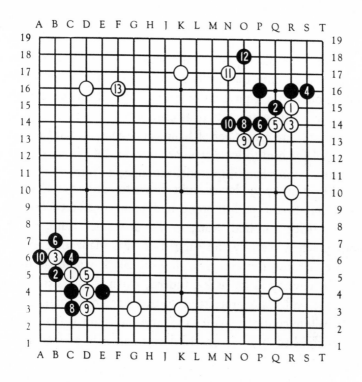

DIAGRAM 66

66, White might threaten an invasion of the corner with 11.m17 and, after 12.n18, obtain fair prospects of building up territory along the upper edge with 13.h17. But after 14.q12; 15.q13, r9 Black would entrench himself solidly along the right side with either r6 or r12, robbing the White group on lines 13, 14, and 15 of all developing potential.

[195]

The lower half of Diagram 66 shows the development which Black would choose if White made the direct attack just discussed with a solid position along the edge already established.

In this case Black permits the separation of his two stones on c4 and e4, thus materially reducing the size of his corner, but he builds up a position of great potential on the left side.

The student, when pitted against stronger players, will invariably receive a number of handicap stones. It will therefore be useful for him to have standard attacks, which are directed against a corner handicap stone, explained to him.

The proper width of side extensions In Diagram 67 the lower right shows the sequence of moves which up to the eighth stone had been considered best for two or three hundred years, so that it seemed quite revolutionary when recently the suggestion was made that instead of safeguarding the corner with 8.o4, Black would do much better extending as far as k3. Indeed, when White answers o4 with 9.l3, and Black protects his territory against invasion with 10.l3, White continues with 11.f3, and the result is that White has established himself on the lower left side as well as on the right.

A Black extension as far as line k, as illustrated in the upper left of the Diagram, must, of course, be justified by showing that White can neither successfully cut through at d15 nor safely invade Black's territory at f17.

When, in answer to the latter move, Black closes his corner with 3.e17 and White extends toward the centre with f16, Black connects at d15 and White finds himself in a most undesirable situation. While extending further toward the centre in order to avoid the surrounding of his two men, White will be pressed by a downward extension of Black's man on line k, and this will at the same time offer Black an opportunity to consolidate a very large territory in the upper right.

[196]

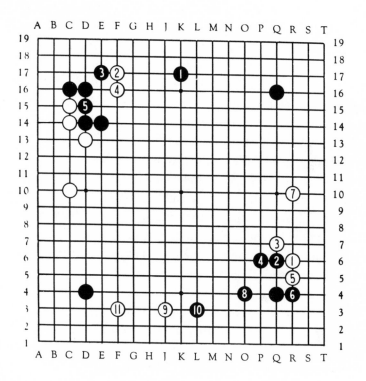

DIAGRAM 67

Let us now examine why, when Black extends as far as k17, White's cut 1.d15 is not a valid threat. Diagram 68 shows the sequence of moves which would refute White's attack.

After stopping White with e15, permitting 3.e16, Black would first play b16, and in reply to 5.b15 continue with c13; 7.b13, c12, which would still be Sente, as a15 followed by b12 would capture the White group. White would defend with 9.b12, and Black would then go after the man on e16 with f16. After 11.e17, f17; 13.d18, f18, as so often in these hand-to-hand fights, it is the difference of a single play which determines victory or defeat. It looks as if White can seal Black's fate with 15.b18, as after c18; 17.c19, e18; 19.d17, c17; 21.d19 Black is left with only two liberties while 22.e19 followed by 23.b19 gives White three breathing spaces. But Black robs White of one of these by first sacrificing a man on b19. After 23.a19*, e19; 25.b19 White also has only two liberties, and since it is Black's move, he wins the White army with 26.b17.

In the position at the lower right of Diagram 68, since the play just illustrated shows that Black does not have to fear the cut q5-p4, he could, instead of extending to k3 right away, try to build a higher wall on the right first, with Sente through a threat to invade White's territory, and then play k3 with much greater advantage.

If he started with 1.q9, r9; 3.q8, and White answered r8, he would indeed accomplish his plan as 5.p7 would force White to lose a move protecting his man on q7. But White would play 4.r7, and now 5.p7, which Black must answer to stop White from breaking out, would not be Sente, so that White could freely invade the lower side.

The best way for Black to carry out his plan would be to play 1.q8, r8; 3.p7. Now White must connect at r7, and Black can occupy k3. The fact that White could then cut at p8 would not have to deter Black. He would reply o8, and after White captures at q9, he would either continue with o9 or make a play tightening his hold on the territory along the lower edge.

The lower left of the Diagram shows an example of the invasion of a corner when Black does not answer the confrontation of his handicap stone by White's c6 but plays else-

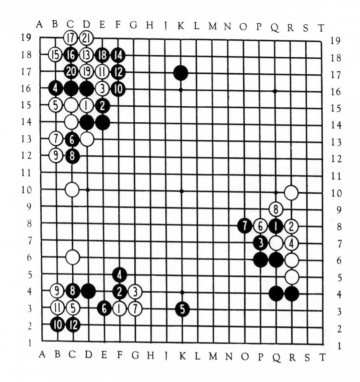

DIAGRAM 68

where on the board. 1.f3 produces a symmetrical position (butterfly) so that it does not make any difference whether Black answers 2.d6 or 2.f4 if no White stones are close by on the side or the lower edge. After the sequence illustrated in the Diagram, White has Sente, as he should have, having started with two men against one.

The student should understand that the handicap stone alone does not prevent the invasion of the corner, even if White has not yet confronted the stone from the outside. In the position shown in Diagram 69, White could immediately occupy r3 and form a safe group worth about ten points. Observing the effect of the series of moves given in the Diagram, one concludes that Black would have been better off had his outposts been placed at k3 and r10 instead of at l3 and r9, because his potential territory would have been larger.

The upper left of the Diagram shows this case, with Black stones added at k15 and e10. If White could not invade the corner, Black's prospective territory would be at least fifty or sixty points. But White could, of course, proceed exactly as in the lower right corner, since the added Black stones on the outside do not affect that procedure. The result is that Black's prospective territory is reduced to about thirty points. White has gained ten points and retained Sente. Thus, he has actually gained about thirty points through his invasion.

It would be bad for White to start the attack on the corner from the outside, as illustrated in the lower left of Diagram 69. (The stones at c10 and e10 as well as those at k3 and k5 are to be considered part of the position.) Black would answer White's 1.c6 with 2.c5, closing off his corner, and after countering 3.d6 with f4 he would control about thirty points along the lower side of the board, while White's two invading stones would lack a base at the edge and would have to fight for their lives.

The situation would be different if, as illustrated in the upper right of the Diagram, one of Black's wing stones were one line farther removed. (Black's position is to be considered as consisting of the three men at q16, k17, and r9.) Here 1.r14 would be the proper start of the attack, particularly if no plays

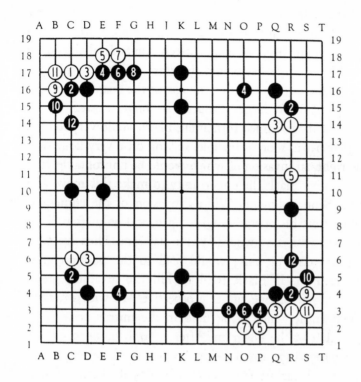

DIAGRAM 69

have as yet been made in the lower right quadrant. After Black's reply r15 and the continuation 3.q14, o16, White would establish a safe base on the right side with 5.r11 with good prospects of successfully invading the corner at an opportune moment with r17 or separating Black's men in the lower right by playing r6 or r7.

Even if Black has already made the customary two-point extension from his handicap stone, as shown in Diagram 70, White can still invade the corner and build a small safe position, robbing Black of about fifteen points. In doing so, White would lose Sente. He would therefore embark on this invasion only if the development on the rest of the board has progressed to a point where larger prospects no longer existed.

In the diagrammed formation, Black would very likely want to play p10 as soon as feasible, staking off a very large space on the right, an invasion of which would be unprofitable. In order not to give Black the opportunity to make this move after he gains Sente following White's invasion of the corner, White would start his operation with 1.p10, and only after Black has guarded with 2.q8 would White play 3.r3. Then r4; 5.q2, o2; 7.s4, s5; 9.s2, t4; 11.s3 would lead to the position given in Diagram 70. If Black tried to kill the invading group by depriving it of one of its prospective Me with r1, the play would ensue which is pictured in the mirror position in the upper left of the Diagram. After 1.c19, b19; 3.d19, e18; 5.e19, f17; 7.g17, e17; 9.g18 White escapes with 10.e16, as 11.e15 would fail against f15 followed by d15 if Black defends the man on f16.

The question might be asked why Black could not play 6.q3 in the lower right, rather than o2. The reason is that after 7.s2, p2; 9.s4, s5, if White has more valid Ko threats on the board than Black, he would not be compelled to make eyes now with 11.t3 or r1, but he could take Sente elsewhere and permit Black to atttack the corner group with q1 or t4.

If Black's outpost were at q10 instead of r10, it would be much easier for White to establish himself on the right side. He would begin with 1.r8, threatening a squeeze play against q10 from above, and after 2.r9; 3.q8, o10 he could continue

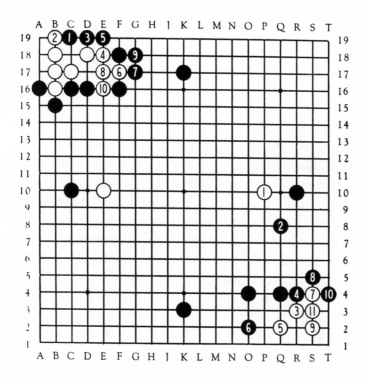

DIAGRAM 70

with 5.s4. This would enable him to build a safe position either in the corner or on the right side. An attempt to kill White with 6.r4; 7.s3, s5 would fail, as the cut 9.r5 would either win Black's man on s5 or, after 10.r6, 11.q5, s6, permit 13.p4, when 14.p5; 15.q6, p3*; 17.r7 would lead to the capture of the men around s6.

[203]

The examples discussed in this chapter will have given the reader a fair insight into the strategic considerations which underlie the proper choice of moves in the opening, the phase of the game which is apt to exert a greater influence upon the final outcome of the struggle than local tactical skirmishes in the middle game. The examples will also have made the student realize that careful calculation of the different variations possible in hand-to-hand encounters is indispensable for the correct evaluation of the continuation selected.

The understanding of the strategic principles, coupled with just enough practice to enable going through the calculation of a combination without glaring errors, will raise the playing strength of the student to a level where he can conduct an intelligent game and make the fight interesting even for players of rank, as long as he receives a handicap which offers approximately equal winning chances to him and to his opponent. Playing with stronger players is the best way to improve one's game rapidly and to arrive at a full comprehension of the opportunities it offers for exciting flights of the imagination.

« 5 »
THE GAME OF GO-MOKU

Go-Moku, called Pegety by one and Ren-ju by another manu- *The rules of the game* facturer who brought the game out in this country, is played with the same equipment as Go.

"Go" in this instance means five, and "Moku" means stones. The object of the game is to get five adjoining stones in a row, either vertically or horizontally or diagonally. Play starts on the vacant board, just as in Go. Black always starts, and the players place a stone alternately on any point of intersection. The game is won only when a player forms a line of *exactly* five of his stones. Making a move which lines up *more* than five of his men contiguously does not count as a victory for him.

It is evident that as soon as a player gets four adjoining stones in a row which is open on either side, he wins the game because his opponent can stop him from forming a five only on one side and he can then complete the five on the other. Thus, in Diagram 71, Black wins by playing 1.f4. If White stops the five on c7, Black completes it on h2, and vice versa.

Consequently, a player threatens to win the game whenever he gets three men in a row in such a way that on the next move he could form a four which is open on both sides. It is customary to call "three" in such a case so that the opponent may not

[205]

forget to stop the formation of the open four, because there is no fun in winning a game owing to a blunder of the adversary; at least there should not be. The idea is to win the game in spite of the opponent's seeing every threat. This can be accomplished only if two threats are made simultaneously, for if only one four or one five is threatened the opponent can always block it.

To arrive at a double threat one would have to form either two fours simultaneously, or two threes which both lead to open fours, or a four and an open three. Diagram 71 shows an example for every one of these cases. By playing 1. f11 Black forms two fours, and White can stop only one. In the position on the upper left either player would win by playing f17, forming two open threes. If the opponent stops one of them, the other will be developed into a four which is open on both sides. On the upper right Black wins with 1.n16, which forms a four and a three; after White stops the four, the three is developed into a four at l 14 or p 18.

The rule of three and three

After a few practice games it becomes evident that the opportunity to form a double three arises in almost every game at a very early stage. This way of winning is considered too easy in the Orient, and there the rule is adhered to that a double three may not be formed if both threes are capable of developing into an open four. In master games, sometimes, only Black is thus restricted, to offset the advantage he has by moving first.

In the upper left corner, accordingly, Black would first play c17, threatening c15, and when White answers c15 Black will continue with f17, forming a four and a three and thus winning.

The move c17 is permissible because one of the two threes which it forms cannot be developed on the next move into a four which is open on both ends.

This rule of three and three need not be adopted by beginners. Experienced players will prefer it. It leads to curious com-

[206]

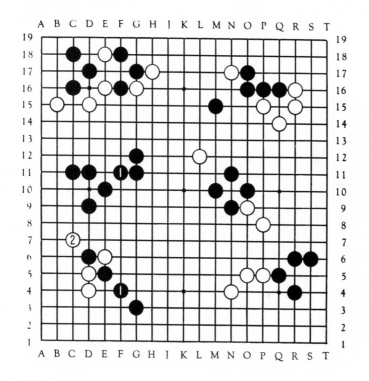

DIAGRAM 71

binations. In the position on the lower right, for instance, neither Black nor White could occupy p6, because two open threes would be formed by that move. Black, on the move, would win the game by first playing o7. White, since he is not permitted to play p6, must stop the threatened four either by s3 or by n8. Then Black plays p6, forming a four and a three, and White is lost.

Similarly, White on the move would start with q7, forcing either m3 or r8, and then he would form a four and three by p6 and win.

When the rule of three and three is adopted, a player is not expected to obey it if the opponent threatens to make a five which can be blocked only by a move that forms two open threes. Thus, in the position of Diagram 71, Black would be permitted to play n10 if White forces that move by the threat m11, and the resulting two open threes would win the game for Black.

In starting the game Black usually places his man on k 10 which leaves an equal amount of space for development in all directions. For the following examples of actual games other first moves have been chosen merely to permit illustrating them in the same diagram. It will be noted that comparatively few moves suffice to produce positions involving double threats.

GAME NO. I

Black	White
1. f 6	h 7
3. h 5	g 5
5. g 6	h 6
7. f 7	i 4

A three was open, and the formation of an open four had to be blocked either by i4 or by e8.

9. e 6	i 7

This is not good because in blocking this three Black opens one himself so that White must answer and the initiative passes back to Black again.

11. f 4	f 5

Black can now force the win with e5, because that move

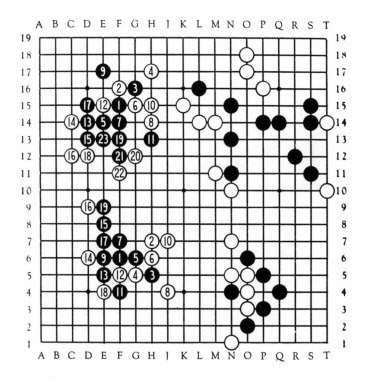

DIAGRAM 72

threatens to form a four and three at d6 as well as at e8. It follows that White should have played e8 on his eighth move rather than i4, but this was difficult to foresee. A little experience would supply the right "feeling" in such a case. The alternative e8 was preferable because it prevented the massing of Black men in that neighbourhood.

[209]

] 13.	e 5	d 6
15.	e 8	d 9
17.	e 7, forming an open four	

GAME NO. 2

1.	f 15	f 16
3.	g 16	h 17
5.	e 14	g 15

More promising would seem 6.e17, forming two rows of two stones each which might be extended into a three at an opportune moment with Sente.

7.	f 14	h 14
9.	e 17	h 15
11.	h 13	e 15

d14 looks much more plausible, as it would keep Black from forming an open three in the fourteenth line. The sequence shows how valuable this point is for Black.

13.	d 14	c 14
15.	d 13	c 12
17.	d 15	d 12
19.	f 13	g 12

Since his inadequate twelfth move White has not had time to breathe. On every turn he was forced to block the threat of an open four. He now succumbs to an easily formed open four-three.

21.	f 12	f 11
23.	e 13, winning.	

The position shown in the upper right of Diagram 72 shows at the first glance that the opposing parties were beginners. White

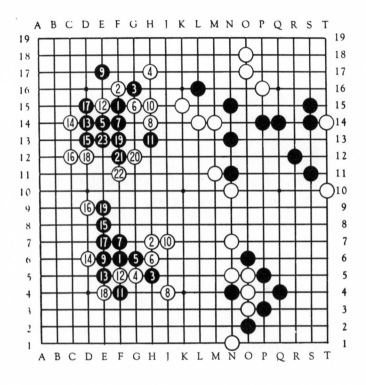

DIAGRAM 72

has done nothing to intertwine his men with those of his adversary, so that the latter can form threes and fours at will, arriving quickly at a double threat which cannot be met.

1.	o 14	r	14
3.	s 13	s	12
5.	p 13		

Now White must stop Black's open three either on q12 or on m16, and then follows 7.r15, 012; 9.s16, forming a double four.

The position in the lower right of the Diagram, also from a beginner's game, is already lost for White. Black's group can expand freely every which way into the territory on its left. The symmetrical array of Black's men suggests continuing the symmetrical shape until the opportunity for a double threat arises:

1.   r 4   r 5

Black threatened to form a four first at r5 and then at r3, thus producing an open three in line r with himself on the move.

3.   p 4   p 6
5.   s 5   p 2
7.   s 4   t 4
9.   s 2, forming a four and an
              open three.

Had White played 4.p2 instead of p6, the winning moves would have been mirror pictures of those just given: 5.s3, 7.s4, and 9.s6.

RECOMMENDED READING

For Beginners:

MORRIS, LESTER and MORRIS, ELISABETH: *The Game of Go,* New York, 1951. Published by the American Go Association.

ROSENTHAL, GILBERT: *13 Line Go.* Booklet published by its author at 4009 Liberty Heights Avenue, Baltimore, Md.

SMITH, ARTHUR: *The Game of Go,* New York, 1908. Reprinted by Charles E. Tuttle, Rutland, Vermont, 1956.

TAKAGAWA, KAKU: *How to Play Go,* Tokyo, 1958.

For Beginners and Advanced Players:

GOODELL, JOHN D.: *The Game of Ki,* 606 Bonifant, Silver Spring, Maryland.

For Advanced Players:

TAKAGAWA, KAKU: *The Vital Points of Go,* Tokyo, 1958.

INDEX

CATALOGUE OF DOVER BOOKS

Chess, Checkers, Games, Go

THE ADVENTURE OF CHESS, Edward Lasker. A lively history of chess, from its ancient beginnings in the Indian 4-handed game of Chaturanga, through to the great players of our day, as told by one of America's finest masters. He introduces such unusual sidelights and amusing oddities as Maelzel's chess-playing automaton that beat Napoleon 3 times. Major discussion of chess-playing machines and personal memories of Nimzovich, Capablanca, etc. 5-page chess primer. 11 illustrations, 53 diagrams. 296pp. 5⅜ x 8.   S510 Paperbound **$1.45**

A TREASURY OF CHESS LORE, edited by Fred Reinfeld. A delightful collection of anecdotes, short stories, aphorisms by and about the masters, poems, accounts of games and tournaments, photography. Hundreds of humorous, pithy, satirical, wise, and historical episodes, comments, and word portraits. A fascinating "must" for chess players; revealing and perhaps seductive to those who wonder what their friends see in the game. 48 photographs (14 full page plates) 12 diagrams. xi + 306pp. 5⅜ x 8.   T458 Paperbound **$1.75**

HOW DO YOU PLAY CHESS? by Fred Reinfeld. A prominent expert covers every basic rule of chess for the beginner in 86 questions and answers: moves, powers of pieces, rationale behind moves, how to play forcefully, history of chess, and much more. Bibliography of chess publications. 11 board diagrams. 48 pages.   **FREE**

THE PLEASURES OF CHESS, Assiac. Internationally known British writer, influential chess columnist, writes wittily about wide variety of chess subjects: Anderssen's "Immortal Game;" only game in which both opponents resigned at once; psychological tactics of Reshevsky, Lasker; varieties played by masters for relaxation, such as "losing chess;" sacrificial orgies; etc. These anecdotes, witty observations will give you fresh appreciation of game. 43 problems. 150 diagrams. 139pp. 5⅜ x 8.   T597 Paperbound **$1.25**

WIN AT CHESS, F. Reinfeld. 300 practical chess situations from actual tournament play to sharpen your chess eye and test your skill. Traps, sacrifices, mates, winning combinations, subtle exchanges, show you how to WIN AT CHESS. Short notes and tables of solutions and alternative moves help you evaluate your progress. Learn to think ahead playing the "crucial moments" of historic games. 300 diagrams. Notes and solutions. Formerly titled CHESS QUIZ. vi + 120pp. 5⅜ x 8.   T438 Paperbound **$1.00**

THE ART OF CHESS, James Mason. An unabridged reprinting of the latest revised edition of the most famous general study of chess ever written. Also included, a complete supplement by Fred Reinfeld, "How Do You Play Chess?", invaluable to beginners for its lively question and answer method. Mason, an early 20th century master, teaches the beginning and intermediate player more than 90 openings, middle game, end game, how to see more moves ahead, to plan purposefully, attack, sacrifice, defend, exchange, and govern general strategy. Supplement. 448 diagrams. 1947 Reinfeld-Bernstein text. Bibliography. xvi + 340pp. 5⅜ x 8.   T463 Paperbound **$1.85**

THE PRINCIPLES OF CHESS, James Mason. This "great chess classic" (N. Y. Times) is a general study covering all aspects of the game: basic forces, resistance, obstruction, opposition, relative values, mating, typical end game situations, combinations, much more. The last section discusses openings, with 50 games illustrating modern master play of Rubinstein, Spielmann, Lasker, Capablanca, etc., selected and annotated by Fred Reinfeld. Will improve the game of any intermediate-skilled player, but is so forceful and lucid that an absolute beginner might use it to become an accomplished player. 1946 Reinfeld edition. 166 diagrams. 378pp. 5⅜ x 8.   T646 Paperbound **$1.85**

LASKER'S MANUAL OF CHESS, Dr. Emanuel Lasker. Probably the greatest chess player of modern times, Dr. Emanuel Lasker held the world championship 28 years, independent of passing schools or fashions. This unmatched study of the game, chiefly for intermediate to skilled players, analyzes basic methods, combinations, position play, the aesthetics of chess, dozens of different openings, etc., with constant reference to great modern games. Contains a brilliant exposition of Steinitz's important theories. Introduction by Fred Reinfeld. Tables of Lasker's tournament record. 3 indices. 308 diagrams. 1 photograph. xxx + 349pp. 5⅜ x 8.   T640 Paperbound **$2.00**

THE ART OF CHESS COMBINATION, E. Znosko-Borovsky. Proves that combinations, perhaps the most aesthetically satisfying, successful technique in chess, can be an integral part of your game, instead of a haphazard occurrence. Games of Capablanca, Rubinstein, Nimzovich, Bird, etc. grouped according to common features, perceptively analyzed to show that every combination begins in certain simple ideas. Will help you to plan many moves ahead. Technical terms almost completely avoided. "In the teaching of chess he may claim to have no superior," P. W. Sergeant. Introduction. Exercises. Solutions. Index. 223pp. 5⅜ x 8.   T583 Paperbound **$1.45**

CATALOGUE OF DOVER BOOKS

MODERN IDEAS IN CHESS, Richard Reti. An enduring classic, because of its unrivalled explanation of the way master chess had developed in the past hundred years. Reti, who was an outstanding theoretician and player, explains each advance in chess by concentrating on the games of the single master most closely associated with it: Morphy, Anderssen, Steinitz, Lasker, Alekhine, other world champions. Play the games in this volume, study Reti's perceptive observations, and have a living picture of the road chess has travelled. Introduction. 34 diagrams. 192pp. 5⅜ x 8.   T638 Paperbound **$1.25**

THE BOOK OF THE NEW YORK INTERNATIONAL CHESS TOURNAMENT, 1924, annotated by A. Alekhine and edited by H. Helms. Long a rare collector's item, this is the book of one of the most brilliant tournaments of all time, during which Capablanca, Lasker, Alekhine, Reti, and others immeasurably enriched chess theory in a thrilling contest. All 110 games played, with Alekhine's unusually penetrating notes. 15 photographs. xi + 271pp. 5⅜ x 8.
T752 Paperbound **$1.85**

KERES' BEST GAMES OF CHESS, selected, annotated by F. Reinfeld. 90 best games, 1931-1948, by one of boldest, most exciting players of modern chess. Games against Alekhine, Bogolyubov, Capablanca, Euwe, Fine, Reshevsky, other masters, show his treatments of openings such as Giuoco Piano, Alekhine Defense, Queen's Gambit Declined; attacks, sacrifices, alternative methods. Preface by Keres gives personal glimpses, evaluations of rivals. 110 diagrams. 272pp. 5⅜ x 8.   T593 Paperbound **$1.35**

HYPERMODERN CHESS as developed in the games of its greatest exponent, ARON NIMZOVICH, edited by Fred Reinfeld. An intensely original player and analyst, Nimzovich's extraordinary approaches startled and often angered the chess world. This volume, designed for the average player, shows in his victories over Alekhine, Lasker, Marshall, Rubinstein, Spielmann, and others, how his iconoclastic methods infused new life into the game. Use Nimzovich to invigorate your play and startle opponents. Introduction. Indices of players and openings. 180 diagrams. viii + 220pp. 5⅜ x 8.   T448 Paperbound **$1.35**

THE DEVELOPMENT OF A CHESS GENIUS: 100 INSTRUCTIVE GAMES OF ALEKHINE, F. Reinfeld. 100 games of the chess giant's formative years, 1905-1914, from age 13 to maturity, each annotated and commented upon by Fred Reinfeld. Included are matches against Bogolyubov, Capablanca, Tarrasch, and many others. You see the growth of an inexperienced genius into one of the greatest players of all time. Many of these games have never appeared before in book form. "One of America's most significant contributions to the chess world," Chess Life. New introduction. Index of players, openings. 204 illustrations. xv +227pp. 5¾ x 8.
T551 Paperbound **$1.35**

RESHEVSKY'S BEST GAMES OF CHESS, Samuel Reshevsky. One time 4-year-old chess genius, 5-time winner U. S. Chess Championship, selects, annotates 110 of his best games, illustrating theories, favorite methods of play against Capablanca, Alekhine, Bogolyubov, Kashdan, Vidmar, Botvinnik, others. Clear, non-technical style. Personal impressions of opponents, autobiographical material, tournament match record. Formerly "Reshevsky on Chess." 309 diagrams, 2 photos. 288pp. 5⅜ x 8.   T606 Paperbound **$1.25**

ONE HUNDRED SELECTED GAMES, Mikhail Botvinnik. Author's own choice of his best games before becoming World Champion in 1948, beginning with first big tournament, the USSR Championship, 1927. Shows his great power of analysis as he annotates these games, giving strategy, technique against Alekhine, Capablanca, Euwe, Keres, Reshevsky, Smyslov, Vidmar, many others. Discusses his career, methods of play, system of training. 6 studies of endgame positions. 221 diagrams. 272pp. 5⅜ x 8.   T620 Paperbound **$1.50**

RUBINSTEIN'S CHESS MASTERPIECES, selected, annotated by Hans Kmoch. Thoroughgoing mastery of opening, middle game; faultless technique in endgame, particularly rook and pawn endings; ability to switch from careful positional play to daring combinations; all distinguish the play of Rubinstein. 100 best games, against Janowski, Nimzowitch, Tarrasch, Vidmar, Capablanca, other greats, carefully annotated, will improve your game rapidly. Biographical introduction, B. F. Winkelman. 103 diagrams. 192pp. 5⅜ x 8.
T617 Paperbound **$1.25**

TARRASCH'S BEST GAMES OF CHESS, selected & annotated by Fred Reinfeld. First definitive collection of games by Siegbert Tarrasch, winner of 7 international tournaments, and the leading theorist of classical chess. 183 games cover fifty years of play against Mason, Mieses, Paulsen, Teichmann, Pillsbury, Janwoski, others. Reinfeld includes Tarrasch's own analyses of many of these games. A careful study and replaying of the games will give you a sound understanding of classical methods, and many hours of enjoyment. Introduction. Indexes. 183 diagrams. xxiv + 386pp. 5⅜ x 8.   T644 Paperbound **$2.00**

MARSHALL'S BEST GAMES OF CHESS, F. J. Marshall. Grandmaster, U. S. Champion for 27 years, tells story of career; presents magnificent collection of 140 of best games, annotated by himself. Games against Alekhine, Capablanca, Emanuel Lasker, Janowski, Rubinstein, Pillsbury, etc. Special section analyzes openings such as King's Gambit, Ruy Lopez, Alekhine's Defense, Giuoco Piano, others. A study of Marshall's brilliant offensives, slashing attacks, extraordinary sacrifices, will rapidly improve your game. Formerly "My Fifty Years of Chess." Introduction. 19 diagrams. 13 photos. 250pp. 5⅜ x 8.   T604 Paperbound **$1.45**

THE HASTINGS CHESS TOURNAMENT, 1895, edited by Horace F. Cheshire. This is the complete tournament book of the famous Hastings 1895 tournament. One of the most exciting tournaments ever to take place, it evoked the finest play from such players as Dr. Lasker, Steinitz, Tarrasch, Harry Pillsbury, Mason, Tchigorin, Schlecter, and others. It was not only extremely exciting as an event, it also created first-rate chess. This book contains fully annotated all 230 games, full information about the playing events, biographies of the players, and much other material that makes it a chess classic. 22 photos, 174 diagrams. x + 370pp. 5⅝ x 8½.   T288 Paperbound **$2.00**

THE BOOK OF THE NOTTINGHAM INTERNATIONAL CHESS TOURNAMENT, 1936, Annotated by Dr. Alexander Alekhine. The Nottingham 1936 tournament is regarded by many chess enthusiasts as the greatest tournament of recent years. It brought together all the living former world champions, the current chess champion, and the future world champion: Dr. Lasker, Capablanca, Alekhine, Euwe, Botvinnik, and Reshevsky, Fine, Flohr, Tartakover, Vidmar, and Bogoljubov. The play was brilliant throughout. This volume contains all 105 of the games played, provided with the remarkable annotations of Alekhine. 1 illustration, 121 diagrams. xx + 291pp. 5⅜ x 8½.   T189 Paperbound **$1.85**

CHESS FOR FUN AND CHESS FOR BLOOD, Edward Lasker. A genial, informative book by one of century's leading masters. Incisive comments on chess as a form of art and recreation, on how a master prepares for and plays a tournament. Best of all is author's move-by-move analysis of his game with Dr. Emanuel Lasker in 1924 World Tournament, a charming and thorough recreation of one of the great games in history: the author's mental processes; how his calculations were upset; how both players blundered; the surprising outcome. Who could not profit from this study-in-depth? For the enthusiast who likes to read about chess as well as play it. Corrected (1942) edition. Preface contains 8 letters to author about the fun of chess. 95 illustrations by Maximilian Mopp. 224pp. 5⅜ x 8½.   T146 Paperbound **$1.25**

HOW NOT TO PLAY CHESS, Eugene A. Znosko-Borovsky. Sticking to a few well-chosen examples and explaining every step along the way, an outstanding chess expositor shows how to avoid playing a hit-or-miss game and instead develop general plans of action based on positional analysis: weak and strong squares, the notion of the controlled square, how to seize control of open lines, weak points in the pawn structure, and so on. Definition and illustration of typical chess mistakes plus 20 problems (from master games) added by Fred Reinfeld for the 1949 edition and a number of good-to-memorize tips make this a lucid book that can teach in a few hours what might otherwise take years to learn. 119pp. 5⅜ x 8.
                                                             T920 Paperbound **$1.00**

THE SOVIET SCHOOL OF CHESS, A. Kotov and M. Yudovich. 128 master games, most unavailable elsewhere, by 51 outstanding players, including Botvinnik, Keres, Smyslov, Tal, against players like Capablanca, Euwe, Reshevsky. All carefully annotated, analyzed. Valuable biographical information about each player, early history of Russian chess, careers and contributions of Chigorin and Alekhine, development of Soviet school from 1920 to present with full over-all study of main features of its games, history of Russian chess literature. The most comprehensive work on Russian chess ever printed, the richest single sourcebook for up-to-date Russian theory and strategy. New introduction. Appendix of Russian Grandmasters, Masters, Master Composers. Two indexes (Players, Games). 30 photographs. 182 diagrams. vi + 390pp. 5⅜ x 8.   T26 Paperbound **$2.00**

THE ART OF THE CHECKMATE, Georges Renaud and Victor Kahn. Two former national chess champions of France examine 127 games, identify 23 kinds of mate, and show the rationale for each. These include Legal's pseudo sacrifice, the double check, the smothered mate, Greco's mate, Morphy's mate, the mate of two bishops, two knights, many, many more. Analysis of ideas, not memorization problems. Review quizzes with answers help readers gauge progress. 80 quiz examples and solutions. 299 diagrams. vi + 208pp.
                                                             T106 Paperbound **$1.35**

HOW TO SOLVE CHESS PROBLEMS, K. S. Howard. Full of practical suggestions for the fan or the beginner—who knows only the moves of the chessmen. Contains preliminary section and 58 two-move, 46 three-move, and 8 four-move problems composed by 27 outstanding American problem creators in the last 30 years. Explanation of all terms and exhaustive index. "Just what is wanted for the student," Brian Harley. 112 problems, solutions. vi +171pp. 5⅜ x 8.
                                                             T748 Paperbound **$1.00**

CHESS STRATEGY, Edward Lasker. Keres, Fine, and other great players have acknowledged their debt to this book, which has taught just about the whole modern school how to play forcefully and intelligently. Covers fundamentals, general strategic principles, middle and end game, objects of attack, etc. Includes 48 dramatic games from master tournaments, all fully analyzed. "Best textbook I know in English," J. R. Capablanca. New introduction by author. Table of openings. Index. 167 illustrations. vii + 282pp. 5⅜ x 8.
                                                             T528 Paperbound **$1.50**

REINFELD ON THE END GAME IN CHESS, F. Reinfeld. Formerly titled PRACTICAL END-GAME PLAY, this book contains clear, simple analyses of 62 end games by such masters as Alekhine, Tarrasch, Marshall, Morphy, Capablanca, and many others. Primary emphasis is on the general principles of transition from middle play to end play. This book is unusual in analyzing weak or incorrect moves to show how error occurs and how to avoid it. Covers king and pawn, minor piece, queen endings, weak squares, centralization, tempo moves, and many other vital factors. 62 diagrams. vi + 177pp. 5⅜ x 8.   T417 Paperbound **$1.25**

CATALOGUE OF DOVER BOOKS

THE AMERICAN TWO-MOVE CHESS PROBLEM, Kenneth S. Howard. One of this country's foremost contemporary problem composers selects an interesting, diversified collection of the best two-movers by 58 top American composers. Involving complete blocks, mutates, three openings and closings, other unusual moves, these problems will help almost any player improve his strategic approach. Probably has no equal for all around artistic excellence, surprising keymoves, interesting strategy. Includes 30-page history of development of American two-mover from Loyd, its founder, to the present. Index of composers. vii + 99pp. 5⅜ x 8½.
T997 Paperbound **$1.00**

WIN AT CHECKERS, M. Hopper. (Formerly CHECKERS). The former World's Unrestricted Checker Champion discusses the principles cf the game, expert's shots and traps, problems for the beginner, standard openings, locating your best move, the end game, opening "blitzkrieg" moves, ways to draw when you are behind your opponent, etc. More than 100 detailed questions and answers anticipate your problems. Appendix. 75 problems with solutions and diagrams. Index. 79 figures. xi + 107pp. 5⅜ x 8. T363 Paperbound **$1.00**

GAMES ANCIENT AND ORIENTAL, AND HOW TO PLAY THEM, E. Falkener. A connoisseur's selection of exciting and different games: Oriental varieties of chess, with unusual pieces and moves (including Japanese shogi); the original pachisi; go; reconstructions of lost Roman and Egyptian games; and many more. Full rules and sample games. Now play at home the games that have entertained millions, not on a fad basis, but for millennia. 345 illustrations and figures. iv + 366pp. 5⅜ x 8. T739 Paperbound **$2.00**

GO AND GO-MOKU, Edward Lasker. A fascinating Oriental game, Go, is winning new devotees in America daily. Rules that you can learn in a few minutes—a wealth of combinations that makes it more profound than chess! This is an easily followed step-by-step explanation of this 2000-year-old game, beginning with fundamentals. New chapter on advanced strategy in this edition! Also contains rules for Go-Moku, a very easy sister game. 72 diagrams. xix + 215pp. 5⅜ x 8. T613 Paperbound **$1.50**

HOW TO FORCE CHECKMATE, F. Reinfeld. Formerly titled CHALLENGE TO CHESSPLAYERS, this is an invaluable collection of 300 lightning strokes selected from actual masters' play, which will demonstrate how to smash your opponent's game with strong decisive moves. No board needed — clear, practical diagrams and easy-to-understand solutions. Learn to plan up to three moves ahead and play a superior end game. 300 diagrams. 111pp. 5⅜ x 8.
T439 Paperbound **$1.25**

CHESSBOARD MAGIC! A COLLECTION OF 160 BRILLIANT ENDINGS, I. Chernev. Contains 160 endgame compositions, all illustrating not only ingenuity of composition, but inherent beauty of solution. In one, five Knights are needed to force mate; in another White forces stalemate though Black finishes eight passed pawns ahead; 150 more, all remarkable, all will sharpen your imagination and increase your skill. "Inexhaustible source of entertainment, an endless feast of delight," Reuben Fine, Grandmaster. Introduction. 160 diagrams. Index of composers. vii + 172pp. 5⅜ x 8. T607 Paperbound **$1.00**

LEARN CHESS FROM THE MASTERS, F. Reinfeld. Formerly titled CHESS BY YOURSELF, this book contains 10 games which you play against such masters as Marshall, Bronstein, Najdorf, and others, and an easy system for grading each move you make against a variety of other possible moves. Detailed annotations reveal the principles of the game through actual play. 91 diagrams. viii + 144pp. 5⅜ x 8. T362 Paperbound **$1.00**

MORPHY'S GAMES OF CHESS, edited by Philip W. Sergeant. You can put boldness into your game by following the brilliant, forceful moves of the man who has been called the greatest chess player of all time. Here are 300 of Morphy's best games carefully annotated to reveal Morphy's principles. 54 classics against masters like Anderssen, Harrwitz, Bird, Paulsen, and others. 52 games at odds; 54 blindfold games; plus over 100 others. Unabridged reissue of the latest revised edition. Bibliography. New introduction by Fred Reinfeld. Annotations and introduction by Sergeant. Index. 235 diagrams. x + 352pp. 5⅜ x 8. T386 Paperbound **$1.85**

CHESS PRAXIS, Aron Nimzovich. Nimzovich was the stormy petrel of chess in the first decades of this century, and his system, known as hypermodern chess, revolutionized all play since his time. Casting aside the classical chess theory of Steinitz and Tarrasch, he created his own analysis of chess, considering dynamic patterns as they emerge during play. This is the fullest exposition of his ideas, and it is easily one of the dozen greatest books ever written on chess. Nimzovich illustrates each of his principles with at least two games, and shows how he applied his concepts successfully in games against such masters as Alekhine, Tarrasch, Reti, Rubinstein, Capablanca, Spielmann and others. Indispensable to every serious chess player. Translated by J. DuMont. 135 diagrams, 1 photo. xi + 364pp. 5½ x 8⅝.
T296 Paperbound **$2.00**

CHESS AND CHECKERS: THE WAY TO MASTERSHIP, Edward Lasker. Complete, lucid instructions for the beginner—and valuable suggestions for the advanced player! For both games the great master and teacher presents fundamentals, elementary tactics, and steps toward becoming a superior player. He concentrates on general principles rather than a mass of rules, comprehension rather than brute memory. Historical introduction. 118 diagrams. xiv + 167pp. 5⅜ x 8. T657 Paperbound **$1.15**

Entertainments, Humor

ODDITIES AND CURIOSITIES OF WORDS AND LITERATURE, C. Bombaugh, edited by M. Gardner. The largest collection of idiosyncratic prose and poetry techniques in English, a legendary work in the curious and amusing bypaths of literary recreations and the play technique in literature—so important in modern works. Contains alphabetic poetry, acrostics, palindromes, scissors verse, centos, emblematic poetry, famous literary puns, hoaxes, notorious slips of the press, hilarious mistranslations, and much more. Revised and enlarged with modern material by Martin Gardner. 368pp. 5⅜ x 8. **T759 Paperbound $1.50**

A NONSENSE ANTHOLOGY, collected by Carolyn Wells. 245 of the best nonsense verses ever written, including nonsense puns, absurd arguments, mock epics and sagas, nonsense ballads, odes, "sick" verses, dog-Latin verses, French nonsense verses, songs. By Edward Lear, Lewis Carroll, Gelett Burgess, W. S. Gilbert, Hilaire Belloc, Peter Newell, Oliver Herford, etc., 83 writers in all plus over four score anonymous nonsense verses. A special section of limericks, plus famous nonsense such as Carroll's "Jabberwocky" and Lear's "The Jumblies" and much excellent verse virtually impossible to locate elsewhere. For 50 years considered the best anthology available. Index of first lines specially prepared for this edition. Introduction by Carolyn Wells. 3 indexes: Title, Author, First lines. xxxiii + 279pp. **T499 Paperbound $1.35**

THE BAD CHILD'S BOOK OF BEASTS, MORE BEASTS FOR WORSE CHILDREN, and A MORAL ALPHA-BET, H. Belloc. Hardly an anthology of humorous verse has appeared in the last 50 years without at least a couple of these famous nonsense verses. But one must see the entire volumes—with all the delightful original illustrations by Sir Basil Blackwood—to appreciate fully Belloc's charming and witty verses that play so subacidly on the platitudes of life and morals that beset his day—and ours. A great humor classic. Three books in one. Total of 157pp. 5⅜ x 8. **T749 Paperbound $1.00**

THE DEVIL'S DICTIONARY, Ambrose Bierce. Sardonic and irreverent barbs puncturing the pomposities and absurdities of American politics, business, religion, literature, and arts, by the country's greatest satirist in the classic tradition. Epigrammatic as Shaw, piercing as Swift, American as Mark Twain, Will Rogers, and Fred Allen, Bierce will always remain the favorite of a small coterie of enthusiasts, and of writers and speakers whom he supplies with "some of the most gorgeous witticisms of the English language" (H. L. Mencken). Over 1000 entries in alphabetical order. 144pp. 5⅜ x 8. **T487 Paperbound $1.00**

THE PURPLE COW AND OTHER NONSENSE, Gelett Burgess. The best of Burgess's early nonsense, selected from the first edition of the "Burgess Nonsense Book." Contains many of his most unusual and truly awe-inspiring pieces: 36 nonsense quatrains, the Poems of Patagonia, Alphabet of Famous Goops, and the other hilarious (and rare) adult nonsense that place him in the forefront of American humorists. All pieces are accompanied by the original Burgess illustrations. 123 illustrations. xiii + 113pp. 5⅜ x 8. **T772 Paperbound $1.00**

MY PIOUS FRIENDS AND DRUNKEN COMPANIONS and MORE PIOUS FRIENDS AND DRUNKEN COMPANIONS, Frank Shay. Folksingers, amateur and professional, and everyone who loves singing: here, available for the first time in 30 years, is this valued collection of 132 ballads, blues, vaudeville numbers, drinking songs, sea chanties, comedy songs. Songs of pre-Beatnik Bohemia; songs from all over America, England, France, Australia; the great songs of the Naughty Nineties and early twentieth-century America. Over a third with music. Woodcuts by John Held, Jr. convey perfectly the brash insouciance of an era of rollicking unabashed song. 12 illustrations by John Held, Jr. Two indexes (Titles and First lines and Choruses). Introductions by the author. Two volumes bound as one. Total of xvi + 235pp. 5⅜ x 8½. **T946 Paperbound $1.25**

HOW TO TELL THE BIRDS FROM THE FLOWERS, R. W. Wood. How not to confuse a carrot with a parrot, a grape with an ape, a puffin with nuffin. Delightful drawings, clever puns, absurd little poems point out far-fetched resemblances in nature. The author was a leading physicist. Introduction by Margaret Wood White. 106 illus. 60pp. 5⅜ x 8. **T523 Paperbound 75¢**

PECK'S BAD BOY AND HIS PA, George W. Peck. The complete edition, containing both volumes, of one of the most widely read American humor books. The endless ingenious pranks played by bad boy "Hennery" on his pa and the grocery man, the outraged pomposity of Pa, the perpetual ridiculing of middle class institutions, are as entertaining today as they were in 1883. No pale sophistications or subtleties, but rather humor vigorous, raw, earthy, imaginative, and, as folk humor often is, sadistic. This peculiarly fascinating book is also valuable to historians and students of American culture as a portrait of an age. 100 original illustrations by True Williams. Introduction by E. F. Bleiler. 347pp. 5⅜ x 8. **T497 Paperbound $1.35**

Puzzles, Mathematical Recreations

SYMBOLIC LOGIC and THE GAME OF LOGIC, Lewis Carroll. "Symbolic Logic" is not concerned with modern symbolic logic, but is instead a collection of over 380 problems posed with charm and imagination, using the syllogism, and a fascinating diagrammatic method of drawing conclusions. In "The Game of Logic" Carroll's whimsical imagination devises a logical game played with 2 diagrams and counters (included) to manipulate hundreds of tricky syllogisms. The final section, "Hit or Miss" is a lagniappe of 101 additional puzzles in the delightful Carroll manner. Until this reprint edition, both of these books were rarities costing up to $15 each. Symbolic Logic: Index. xxxi + 199pp. The Game of Logic: 96pp. 2 vols. bound as one. 5⅜ x 8. **T492 Paperbound $1.50**

PILLOW PROBLEMS and A TANGLED TALE, Lewis Carroll. One of the rarest of all Carroll's works, "Pillow Problems" contains 72 original math puzzles, all typically ingenious. Particularly fascinating are Carroll's answers which remain exactly as he thought them out, reflecting his actual mental process. The problems in "A Tangled Tale" are in story form, originally appearing as a monthly magazine serial. Carroll not only gives the solutions, but uses answers sent in by readers to discuss wrong approaches and misleading paths, and grades them for insight. Both of these books were rarities until this edition, "Pillow Problems" costing up to $25, and "A Tangled Tale" $15. Pillow Problems: Preface and Introduction by Lewis Carroll. xx + 109pp. A Tangled Tale: 6 illustrations. 152pp. Two vols. bound as one. 5⅜ x 8. **T493 Paperbound $1.50**

AMUSEMENTS IN MATHEMATICS, Henry Ernest Dudeney. The foremost British originator of mathematical puzzles is always intriguing, witty, and paradoxical in this classic, one of the largest collections of mathematical amusements. More than 430 puzzles, problems, and paradoxes. Mazes and games, problems on number manipulation, unicursal and other route problems, puzzles on measuring, weighing, packing, age, kinship, chessboards, joiners', crossing river, plane figure dissection, and many others. Solutions. More than 450 illustrations. vii + 258pp. 5⅜ x 8. **T473 Paperbound $1.25**

THE CANTERBURY PUZZLES, Henry Dudeney. Chaucer's pilgrims set one another problems in story form. Also Adventures of the Puzzle Club, the Strange Escape of the King's Jester, the Monks of Riddlewell, the Squire's Christmas Puzzle Party, and others. All puzzles are original, based on dissecting plane figures, arithmetic, algebra, elementary calculus and other branches of mathematics, and purely logical ingenuity. "The limit of ingenuity and intricacy," The Observer. Over 110 puzzles. Full Solutions. 150 illustrations. vii + 225pp. 5⅜ x 8. **T474 Paperbound $1.25**

MATHEMATICAL EXCURSIONS, H. A. Merrill. Even if you hardly remember your high school math, you'll enjoy the 90 stimulating problems contained in this book and you will come to understand a great many mathematical principles with surprisingly little effort. Many useful shortcuts and diversions not generally known are included: division by inspection, Russian peasant multiplication, memory systems for pi, building odd and even magic squares, square roots by geometry, dyadic systems, and many more. Solutions to difficult problems. 50 illustrations. 145pp. 5⅜ x 8. **T350 Paperbound $1.00**

MAGIC SQUARES AND CUBES, W. S. Andrews. Only book-length treatment in English, a thorough non-technical description and analysis. Here are nasik, overlapping, pandiagonal, serrated squares; magic circles, cubes, spheres, rhombuses. Try your hand at 4-dimensional magical figures! Much unusual folklore and tradition included. High school algebra is sufficient. 754 diagrams and illustrations. viii + 419pp. 5⅜ x 8. **T658 Paperbound $1.85**

CALIBAN'S PROBLEM BOOK: MATHEMATICAL, INFERENTIAL AND CRYPTOGRAPHIC PUZZLES, H. Phillips (Caliban), S. T. Shovelton, G. S. Marshall. 105 ingenious problems by the greatest living creator of puzzles based on logic and inference. Rigorous, modern, piquant; reflecting their author's unusual personality, these intermediate and advanced puzzles all involve the ability to reason clearly through complex situations; some call for mathematical knowledge, ranging from algebra to number theory. Solutions. xi + 180pp. 5⅜ x 8. **T736 Paperbound $1.25**

MATHEMATICAL PUZZLES FOR BEGINNERS AND ENTHUSIASTS, G. Mott-Smith. 188 mathematical puzzles based on algebra, dissection of plane figures, permutations, and probability, that will test and improve your powers of inference and interpretation. The Odic Force, The Spider's Cousin, Ellipse Drawing, theory and strategy of card and board games like tit-tat-toe, go moku, salvo, and many others. 100 pages of detailed mathematical explanations. Appendix of primes, square roots, etc. 135 illustrations. 2nd revised edition. 248pp. 5⅜ x 8. **T198 Paperbound $1.00**

MATHEMAGIC, MAGIC PUZZLES, AND GAMES WITH NUMBERS, R. V. Heath. More than 60 new puzzles and stunts based on the properties of numbers. Easy techniques for multiplying large numbers mentally, revealing hidden numbers magically, finding the date of any day in any year, and dozens more. Over 30 pages devoted to magic squares, triangles, cubes, circles, etc. Edited by J. S. Meyer. 76 illustrations. 128pp. 5⅜ x 8. **T110 Paperbound $1.00**

MATHEMATICAL RECREATIONS, M. Kraitchik. One of the most thorough compilations of unusual mathematical problems for beginners and advanced mathematicians. Historical problems from Greek, Medieval, Arabic, Hindu sources. 50 pages devoted to pastimes derived from figurate numbers, Mersenne numbers, Fermat numbers, primes and probability. 40 pages of magic, Euler, Latin, panmagic squares. 25 new positional and permutational games of permanent value: fairy chess, latruncles, reversi, jinx, ruma, lasca, tricolor, tetrachrome, etc. Complete rigorous solutions. Revised second edition. 181 illustrations. 333pp. 5⅜ x 8.
T163 Paperbound **$1.75**

MATHEMATICAL PUZZLES OF SAM LOYD, selected and edited by M. Gardner. Choice puzzles by the greatest American puzzle creator and innovator. Selected from his famous collection, "Cyclopedia of Puzzles," they retain the unique style and historical flavor of the originals. There are posers based on arithmetic, algebra, probability, game theory, route tracing, topology, counter, sliding block, operations research, geometrical dissection. Includes the famous "14-15" puzzle which was a national craze, and his "Horse of a Different Color" which sold millions of copies. 117 of his most ingenious puzzles in all, 120 line drawings and diagrams. Solutions. Selected references. xx + 167pp. 5⅜ x 8.   T498 Paperbound **$1.00**

MATHEMATICAL PUZZLES OF SAM LOYD, Vol. II, selected and edited by Martin Gardner. The outstanding 2nd selection from the great American innovator's "Cyclopedia of Puzzles": speed and distance problems, clock problems, plane and solid geometry, calculus problems, etc. Analytical table of contents that groups the puzzles according to the type of mathematics necessary to solve them. 166 puzzles, 150 original line drawings and diagrams. Selected references. xiv + 177pp. 5⅜ x 8.   T709 Paperbound **$1.00**

ARITHMETICAL EXCURSIONS: AN ENRICHMENT OF ELEMENTARY MATHEMATICS, H. Bowers and J. Bowers. A lively and lighthearted collection of facts and entertainments for anyone who enjoys manipulating numbers or solving arithmetical puzzles: methods of arithmetic never taught in school, little-known facts about the most simple numbers, and clear explanations of more sophisticated topics; mysteries and folklore of numbers, the "Hin-dog-abic" number system, etc. First publication. Index. 529 numbered problems and diversions, all with answers. Bibliography. 60 figures. xiv + 320pp. 5⅜ x 8.   T770 Paperbound **$1.65**

CRYPTANALYSIS, H. F. Gaines. Formerly entitled ELEMENTARY CRYPTANALYSIS, this introductory-intermediate level text is the best book in print on cryptograms and their solution. It covers all major techniques of the past, and contains much that is not generally known except to experts. Full details about concealment, substitution, and transposition ciphers; periodic mixed alphabets, multafid, Kasiski and Vigenere methods, Ohaver patterns, Playfair, and scores of other topics. 6 language letter and word frequency appendix. 167 problems, now furnished with solutions. Index. 173 figures. vi + 230pp. 5⅜ x 8.
T97 Paperbound **$2.00**

CRYPTOGRAPHY, L. D. Smith. An excellent introductory work on ciphers and their solution, the history of secret writing, and actual methods and problems in such techniques as transposition and substitution. Appendices describe the enciphering of Japanese, the Baconian biliteral cipher, and contain frequency tables and a bibliography for further study. Over 150 problems with solutions. 160pp. 5⅜ x 8.   T247 Paperbound **$1.00**

PUZZLE QUIZ AND STUNT FUN, J. Meyer. The solution to party doldrums. 238 challenging puzzles, stunts and tricks. Mathematical puzzles like The Clever Carpenter, Atom Bomb; mysteries and deductions like The Bridge of Sighs, The Nine Pearls, Dog Logic; observation puzzles like Cigarette Smokers, Telephone Dial; over 200 others including magic squares, tongue twisters, puns, anagrams, and many others. All problems solved fully. 250pp. 5⅜ x 8.
T337 Paperbound **$1.00**

101 PUZZLES IN THOUGHT AND LOGIC, C. R. Wylie, Jr. Brand new problems you need no special knowledge to solve! Take the kinks out of your mental "muscles" and enjoy solving murder problems, the detection of lying fishermen, the logical identification of color by a blindman, and dozens more. Introduction with simplified explanation of general scientific method and puzzle solving. 128pp. 5⅜ x 8.   T367 Paperbound **$1.00**

MY BEST PROBLEMS IN MATHEMATICS, Hubert Phillips ("Caliban"). Only elementary mathematics needed to solve these 100 witty, catchy problems by a master problem creator. Problems on the odds in cards and dice, problems in geometry, algebra, permutations, even problems that require no math at all—just a logical mind, clear thinking. Solutions completely worked out. If you enjoy mysteries, alerting your perceptive powers and exercising your detective's eye, you'll find these cryptic puzzles a challenging delight. Original 1961 publication. 100 puzzles, solutions. x + 107pp. 5⅝ x 8.   T91 Paperbound **$1.00**

MY BEST PUZZLES IN LOGIC AND REASONING, Hubert Phillips ("Caliban"). A new collection of 100 inferential and logical puzzles chosen from the best that have appeared in England, available for first time in U.S. By the most endlessly resourceful puzzle creator now living. All data presented are both necessary and sufficient to allow a single unambiguous answer. No special knowledge is required for problems ranging from relatively simple to completely original one-of-a-kinds. Guaranteed to please beginners and experts of all ages. Original publication. 100 puzzles, full solutions. x + 107pp. 5⅜ x 8.   T119 Paperbound **$1.00**

CATALOGUE OF DOVER BOOKS

THE BOOK OF MODERN PUZZLES, G. L. Kaufman. A completely new series of puzzles as fascinating as crossword and deduction puzzles but based upon different principles and techniques. Simple 2-minute teasers, word labyrinths, design and pattern puzzles, logic and observation puzzles — over 150 braincrackers. Answers to all problems. 116 illustrations. 192pp. 5⅜ x 8.
T143 Paperbound **$1.00**

NEW WORD PUZZLES, G. L. Kaufman. 100 ENTIRELY NEW puzzles based on words and their combinations that will delight crossword puzzle, Scrabble and Jotto fans. Chess words, based on the moves of the chess king; design-onyms, symmetrical designs made of synonyms; rhymed double-crostics; syllable sentences; addle letter anagrams; alphagrams; linkograms; and many others all brand new. Full solutions. Space to work problems. 196 figures. vi + 122pp. 5⅜ x 8.
T344 Paperbound **$1.00**

MAZES AND LABYRINTHS: A BOOK OF PUZZLES, W. Shepherd. Mazes, formerly associated with mystery and ritual, are still among the most intriguing of intellectual puzzles. This is a novel and different collection of 50 amusements that embody the principle of the maze: mazes in the classical tradition; 3-dimensional, ribbon, and Möbius-strip mazes; hidden messages; spatial arrangements; etc.—almost all built on amusing story situations. 84 illustrations. Essay on maze psychology. Solutions. xv + 122pp. 5⅜ x 8.
T731 Paperbound **$1.00**

MAGIC TRICKS & CARD TRICKS, W. Jonson. Two books bound as one. 52 tricks with cards, 37 tricks with coins, bills, eggs, smoke, ribbons, slates, etc. Details on presentation, misdirection, and routining will help you master such famous tricks as the Changing Card, Card in the Pocket, Four Aces, Coin Through the Hand, Bill in the Egg, Afghan Bands, and over 75 others. If you follow the lucid exposition and key diagrams carefully, you will finish these two books with an astonishing mastery of magic. 106 figures. 224pp. 5⅜ x 8. T909 Paperbound **$1.00**

PANORAMA OF MAGIC, Milbourne Christopher. A profusely illustrated history of stage magic, a unique selection of prints and engravings from the author's private collection of magic memorabilia, the largest of its kind. Apparatus, stage settings and costumes; ingenious ads distributed by the performers and satiric broadsides passed around in the streets ridiculing pompous showmen; programs; decorative souvenirs. The lively text, by one of America's foremost professional magicians, is full of anecdotes about almost legendary wizards: Dede, the Egyptian; Philadelphia, the wonder-worker; Robert-Houdin, "the father of modern magic;" Harry Houdini; scores more. Altogether a pleasure package for anyone interested in magic, stage setting and design, ethnology, psychology, or simply in unusual people. A Dover original. 295 illustrations; 8 in full color. Index. viii + 216pp. 8⅜ x 11¼.
T774 Paperbound **$2.25**

HOUDINI ON MAGIC, Harry Houdini. One of the greatest magicians of modern times explains his most prized secrets. How locks are picked, with illustrated picks and skeleton keys; how a girl is sawed into twins; how to walk through a brick wall — Houdini's explanations of 44 stage tricks with many diagrams. Also included is a fascinating discussion of great magicians of the past and the story of his fight against fraudulent mediums and spiritualists. Edited by W.B. Gibson and M.N. Young. Bibliography. 155 figures, photos. xv + 280pp. 5⅜ x 8.
T384 Paperbound **$1.25**

MATHEMATICS, MAGIC AND MYSTERY, Martin Gardner. Why do card tricks work? How do magicians perform astonishing mathematical feats? How is stage mind-reading possible? This is the first book length study explaining the application of probability, set theory, theory of numbers, topology, etc., to achieve many startling tricks. Non-technical, accurate, detailed! 115 sections discuss tricks with cards, dice, coins, knots, geometrical vanishing illusions, how a Curry square "demonstrates" that the sum of the parts may be greater than the whole, and dozens of others. No sleight of hand necessary! 135 illustrations. xii + 174pp. 5⅜ x 8.
T335 Paperbound **$1.00**

EASY-TO-DO ENTERTAINMENTS AND DIVERSIONS WITH COINS, CARDS, STRING, PAPER AND MATCHES, R. M. Abraham. Over 300 tricks, games and puzzles will provide young readers with absorbing fun. Sections on card games; paper-folding; tricks with coins, matches and pieces of string; games for the agile; toy-making from common household objects; mathematical recreations; and 50 miscellaneous pastimes. Anyone in charge of groups of youngsters, including hard-pressed parents, and in need of suggestions on how to keep children sensibly amused and quietly content will find this book indispensable. Clear, simple text, copious number of delightful line drawings and illustrative diagrams. Originally titled "Winter Nights Entertainments." Introduction by Lord Baden Powell. 329 illustrations. v + 186pp. 5⅜ x 8½.
T921 Paperbound **$1.00**

STRING FIGURES AND HOW TO MAKE THEM, Caroline Furness Jayne. 107 string figures plus variations selected from the best primitive and modern examples developed by Navajo, Apache, pygmies of Africa, Eskimo, in Europe, Australia, China, etc. The most readily understandable, easy-to-follow book in English on perennially popular recreation. Crystal-clear exposition; step-by-step diagrams. Everyone from kindergarten children to adults looking for unusual diversion will be endlessly amused. Index. Bibliography. Introduction by A. C. Haddon. 17 full-page plates. 960 illustrations. xxiii + 401pp. 5⅜ x 8½.
T152 Paperbound **$2.00**

Fiction

THE LAND THAT TIME FORGOT and THE MOON MAID, Edgar Rice Burroughs. In the opinion of many, Burroughs' best work. The first concerns a strange island where evolution is individual rather than phylogenetic. Speechless anthropoids develop into intelligent human beings within a single generation. The second projects the reader far into the future and describes the first voyage to the Moon (in the year 2025), the conquest of the Earth by the Moon, and years of violence and adventure as the enslaved Earthmen try to regain possession of their planet. "An imaginative tour de force that keeps the reader keyed up and expectant," NEW YORK TIMES. Complete, unabridged text of the original two novels (three parts in each). 5 illustrations by J. Allen St. John. vi + 552pp. 5⅜ x 8½.
T1020 Clothbound **$3.75**
T358 Paperbound **$2.00**

AT THE EARTH'S CORE, PELLUCIDAR, TANAR OF PELLUCIDAR: THREE SCIENCE FICTION NOVELS BY EDGAR RICE BURROUGHS. Complete, unabridged texts of the first three Pellucidar novels. Tales of derring-do by the famous master of science fiction. The locale for these three related stories is the inner surface of the hollow Earth where we discover the world of Pellucidar, complete with all types of bizarre, menacing creatures, strange peoples, and alluring maidens—guaranteed to delight all Burroughs fans and a wide circle of adventure lovers. Illustrated by J. Allen St. John and P. F. Berdanier. vi + 433pp. 5⅜ x 8½.
T1051 Paperbound **$2.00**

THREE MARTIAN NOVELS, Edgar Rice Burroughs. Contains: Thuvia, Maid of Mars; The Chessmen of Mars; and The Master Mind of Mars. High adventure set in an imaginative and intricate conception of the Red Planet. Mars is peopled with an intelligent, heroic human race which lives in densely populated cities and with fierce barbarians who inhabit dead sea bottoms. Other exciting creatures abound amidst an inventive framework of Martian history and geography. Complete unabridged reprintings of the first edition. 16 illustrations by J. Allen St. John. vi + 499pp. 5⅜ x 8½.
T39 Paperbound **$1.85**

TO THE SUN? and OFF ON A COMET!, Jules Verne. Complete texts of two of the most imaginative flights into fancy in world literature display the high adventure that have kept Verne's novels read for nearly a century. Only unabridged edition of the best translation, by Edward Roth. Large, easily readable type. 50 illustrations selected from first editions. 462pp. 5⅜ x 8.
T634 Paperbound **$1.75**

FROM THE EARTH TO THE MOON and ALL AROUND THE MOON, Jules Verne. Complete editions of two of Verne's most successful novels, in finest Edward Roth translations, now available after many years out of print. Verne's visions of submarines, airplanes, television, rockets, interplanetary travel; of scientific and not-so-scientific beliefs; of peculiarities of Americans; all delight and engross us today as much as when they first appeared. Large, easily readable type. 42 illus. from first French edition. 476pp. 5⅜ x 8.
T633 Paperbound **$1.75**

THREE PROPHETIC NOVELS BY H. G. WELLS, edited by E. F. Bleiler. Complete texts of "When the Sleeper Wakes" (1st book printing in 50 years), "A Story of the Days to Come," "The Time Machine" (1st complete printing in book form). Exciting adventures in the future are as enjoyable today as 50 years ago when first printed. Predict TV, movies, intercontinental airplanes, prefabricated houses, air-conditioned cities, etc. First important author to foresee problems of mind control, technological dictatorships. "Absolute best of imaginative fiction," N. Y. Times. Introduction. 335pp. 5⅜ x 8.
T605 Paperbound **$1.50**

SEVEN SCIENCE FICTION NOVELS, H. G. Wells. Full unabridged texts of 7 science-fiction novels of the master. Ranging from biology, physics, chemistry, astronomy to sociology and other studies, Mr. Wells extrapolates whole worlds of strange and intriguing character. "One will have to go far to match this for entertainment, excitement, and sheer pleasure . . . ," NEW YORK TIMES. Contents: The Time Machine, The Island of Dr. Moreau, First Men in the Moon, The Invisible Man, The War of the Worlds, The Food of the Gods, In the Days of the Comet. 1015pp. 5⅜ x 8.
T264 Clothbound **$4.50**

28 SCIENCE FICTION STORIES OF H. G. WELLS. Two full unabridged novels, MEN LIKE GODS and STAR BEGOTTEN, plus 26 short stories by the master science-fiction writer of all time. Stories of space, time, invention, exploration, future adventure—an indispensable part of the library of everyone interested in science and adventure. PARTIAL CONTENTS: Men Like Gods, The Country of the Blind, In the Abyss, The Crystal Egg, The Man Who Could Work Miracles, A Story of the Days to Come, The Valley of Spiders, and 21 more! 928pp. 5⅜ x 8.
T265 Clothbound **$4.50**

THE WAR IN THE AIR, IN THE DAYS OF THE COMET, THE FOOD OF THE GODS: THREE SCIENCE FICTION NOVELS BY H. G. WELLS. Three exciting Wells offerings bearing on vital social and philosophical issues of his and our own day. Here are tales of air power, strategic bombing, East vs. West, the potential miracles of science, the potential disasters from outer space, the relationship between scientific advancement and moral progress, etc. First reprinting of "War in the Air" in almost 50 years. An excellent sampling of Wells at his storytelling best. Complete, unabridged reprintings. 16 illustrations. 645pp. 5⅜ x 8½.
T1135 Paperbound **$2.00**

THE PIRATES OF VENUS and LOST ON VENUS: TWO VENUS NOVELS BY EDGAR RICE BURROUGHS.
Two related novels, complete and unabridged. Exciting adventure on the planet Venus with
Earthman Carson Napier broken-field running through one dangerous episode after another.
All lovers of swashbuckling science fiction will enjoy these two stories set in a world of
fascinating societies, fierce beasts, 5000-ft. trees, lush vegetation, and wide seas. Illustra-
tions by Fortunino Matania. Total of vi + 340pp. 5⅜ x 8½. T1053 Paperbound **$1.75**

**A PRINCESS OF MARS and A FIGHTING MAN OF MARS: TWO MARTIAN NOVELS BY EDGAR
RICE BURROUGHS.** "Princess of Mars" is the very first of the great Martian novels written
by Burroughs, and it is probably the best of them all; it set the pattern for all of his later
fantasy novels and contains a thrilling cast of strange peoples and creatures and the
formula of Olympian heroism amidst ever-fluctuating fortunes which Burroughs carries off
so successfully. "Fighting Man" returns to the same scenes and cities—many years later.
A mad scientist, a degenerate dictator, and an indomitable defender of the right clash—
with the fate of the Red Planet at stake! Complete, unabridged reprinting of original editions. Illustrations by F. E. Schoonover and Hugh Hutton. v + 356pp. 5⅜ x 8½.
T1140 Paperbound **$1.75**

RURITANIA COMPLETE: THE PRISONER OF ZENDA and RUPERT OF HENTZAU, Anthony Hope.
The first edition to include in one volume both the continually-popular "Prisoner of Zenda"
and its equally-absorbing sequel. Hope's mythical country of Ruritania has become a household word and the activities of its inhabitants almost a common heritage. Unabridged
reprinting. 14 illustrations by Charles Dana Gibson. vi + 414pp. 5⅜ x 8½.
T69 Paperbound **$1.35**

FLATLAND, E. A. Abbott. A science-fiction classic of life in a 2-dimensional world that is also
a first-rate introduction to such aspects of modern science as relativity and hyperspace.
Political, moral, satirical, and humorous overtones have made FLATLAND fascinating reading
for thousands. 7th edition. New introduction by Banesh Hoffmann. 16 illustrations. 128pp.
5⅜ x 8. T1 Paperbound **$1.00**

THE WONDERFUL WIZARD OF OZ, L. F. Baum. Only edition in print with all the original W. W.
Denslow illustrations in full color—as much a part of "The Wizard" as Tenniel's drawings
are for "Alice in Wonderland." "The Wizard" is still America's best-loved fairy tale, in
which, as the author expresses it, "The wonderment and joy are retained and the heartaches
and nightmares left out." Now today's young readers can enjoy every word and wonderful
picture of the original book. New introduction by Martin Gardner. A Baum bibliography. 23
full-page color plates. viii + 268pp. 5⅜ x 8. T691 Paperbound **$1.50**

THE MARVELOUS LAND OF OZ, L. F. Baum. This is the equally enchanting sequel to the
"Wizard," containing the adventures of the Scarecrow and the Tin Woodman. The hero this
time is a little boy named Tip, and all the delightful Oz magic is still present. This is the
book with the Animated Saw-horse, the Woggle-Bug, and Jack Pumpkinhead. All the original
John R. Neill illustrations, 16 in full color. 287pp. 5⅜ x 8. T692 Paperbound **$1.50**

FIVE GREAT DOG NOVELS, edited by Blanche Cirker. The complete original texts of five classic
dog novels that have delighted and thrilled millions of children and adults throughout the
world with stories of loyalty, adventure, and courage. Full texts of Jack London's "The Call
of the Wild"; John Brown's "Rab and His Friends"; Alfred Ollivant's "Bob, Son of Battle";
Marshall Saunders' "Beautiful Joe"; and Ouida's "A Dog of Flanders." 21 illustrations from
the original editions. 495pp. 5⅜ x 8. T777 Paperbound **$1.75**

THE CASTING AWAY OF MRS. LECKS AND MRS. ALESHINE, F. R. Stockton. A charming light
novel by Frank Stockton, one of America's finest humorists (and author of "The Lady, or the
Tiger?"). This book has made millions of Americans laugh at the reflection of themselves in
two middle-aged American women involved in some of the strangest adventures on record.
You will laugh, too, as they endure shipwreck, desert island, and blizzard with maddening
tranquility. Also contains complete text of "The Dusantes," sequel to "The Casting Away."
49 original illustrations by F. D. Steele. vii + 142pp. 5⅜ x 8. T743 Paperbound **$1.00**

GHOST AND HORROR STORIES OF AMBROSE BIERCE, Selected and introduced by E. F. Bleiler.
24 morbid, eerie tales—the cream of Bierce's fiction output. Contains such memorable
pieces as "The Moonlit Road," "The Damned Thing," "An Inhabitant of Carcosa," "The Eyes
of the Panther," "The Famous Gilson Bequest," "The Middle Toe of the Right Foot," and
other chilling stories, plus the essay, "Visions of the Night" in which Bierce gives us a
kind of rationale for his aesthetic of horror. New collection (1964). xxii + 199pp. 5⅜ x
8⅜. T767 Paperbound **$1.00**

BEST GHOST STORIES OF J. S. LE FANU, Selected and introduced by E. F. Bleiler. LeFanu is
deemed the greatest name in Victorian supernatural fiction. Here are 16 of his best horror
stories, including 2 nouvelles: "Carmilla," a classic vampire tale couched in a perverse
eroticism, and "The Haunted Baronet." Also: "Sir Toby's Will," "Green Tea," "Schalken the
Painter," "Ultor de Lacy," "The Familiar," etc. The first American publication of about half
of this material: a long-overdue opportunity to get a choice sampling of LeFanu's work. New
selection (1964). 8 illustrations. 5⅜ x 8⅜. T415 Paperbound **$1.85**

Dover Classical Records

Now available directly to the public exclusively from Dover: top-quality recordings of fine classical music for only $2 per record! Almost all were released by major record companies to sell for $5 and $6. These recordings were issued under our imprint only after they had passed a severe critical test. We insisted upon:

First-rate music that is enjoyable, musically important and culturally significant.

First-rate performances, where the artists have carried out the composer's intentions, in which the music is alive, vigorous, played with understanding and sensitivity.

First-rate sound—clear, sonorous, fully balanced, crackle-free, whir-free.

Have in your home music by major composers, performed by such gifted musicians as Elsner, Gitlis, Wührer, Beveridge Webster, the Barchet Quartet, Gimpel, etc. Enthusiastically received when first released, many of these performances are definitive. The records are not seconds or remainders, but brand new pressings made on pure vinyl from carefully chosen master tapes. "All purpose" 12″ monaural 33⅓ rpm records, they play equally well on hi-fi and stereo equipment. Fine music for discriminating music lovers, superlatively played, flawlessly recorded: there is no better way to build your library of recorded classical music at remarkable savings. There are no strings; this is not a come-on, not a club, forcing you to buy records you may not want in order to get a few at a lower price. Buy whatever records you want in any quantity, and never pay more than $2 each. Your obligation ends with your first purchase. And that's when ours begins. Dover's money-back guarantee allows you to return any record for any reason, even if you don't like the music, for a full, immediate refund—no questions asked.

MOZART: STRING QUARTETS: IN A (K. 464) AND C ("DISSONANT") (K. 465), Barchet Quartet. The final two of the famous Haydn Quartets, high-points in the history of music. The A Major was accepted with delight by Mozart's contemporaries, but the C Major, with its dissonant opening, aroused strong protest. Today, of course, the remarkable resolutions of the dissonances are recognized as major musical achievements. "Beautiful warm playing," MUSICAL AMERICA. "Two of Mozart's loveliest quartets in a distinguished performance," REV. OF RECORDED MUSIC. (Playing time 58 mins.) HCR 5200 **$2.00**

MOZART: STRING QUARTETS: IN G (K. 80), D (K. 156), and C (K. 157), Barchet Quartet. The early chamber music of Mozart receives unfortunately little attention. First-rate music of the Italian school, it contains all the lightness and charm that belongs only to the youthful Mozart. This is currently the only separate source for the composer's work of this period. "Excellent," HIGH FIDELITY. "Filled with sunshine and youthful joy; played with verve, recorded sound live and brilliant," CHRISTIAN SCI. MONITOR. (playing time 51 mins.) HCR 5201 **$2.00**

MOZART: SERENADES: #9 IN D ("POSTHORN") (K. 320), #6 IN D ("SERENATA NOTTURNA") (K. 239), Pro Musica Orch. of Stuttgart, under Edouard van Remoortel. For Mozart, the serenade was a highly effective form, since he could bring to it the immediacy and intimacy of chamber music as well as the free fantasy of larger group music. Both these serenades are distinguished by a playful, mischievous quality, a spirit perfectly captured in this fine performance. "A triumph, polished playing from the orchestra," HI FI MUSIC AT HOME. "Sound is rich and resonant, fidelity is wonderful," REV. OF RECORDED MUSIC. (Playing time 51 mins.) HCR 5202 **$2.00**

MOZART: DIVERTIMENTO FOR VIOLIN, VIOLA AND CELLO IN E FLAT (K. 563); ADAGIO AND FUGUE IN F MINOR (K. 404a), Kehr Trio. The divertimento is one of Mozart's most beloved pieces, called by Einstein "the finest and most perfect trio ever heard." It is difficult to imagine a music lover who will not be delighted by it. This is the only recording of the lesser known Adagio and Fugue, written in 1782 and influenced by Bach's Well-Tempered Clavichord. "Extremely beautiful recording, strongly recommended," THE OBSERVER. "Superior to rival editions," HIGH FIDELITY. (Playing time 51 mins.) HCR 5203 **$2.00**

SCHUMANN: KREISLERIANA (OPUS 16) AND FANTASIA IN C (OPUS 17), Vlado Perlemuter, Piano. The vigorous Romantic imagination and the remarkable emotional qualities of Schumann's piano music raise it to a special eminence in 19th-century creativity. Both these pieces are rooted to the composer's tortuous romance with his future wife, Clara, and both receive brilliant treatment at the hands of Vlado Perlemuter, Paris Conservatory, proclaimed by Alfred Cortot "not only a great virtuoso but also a great musician." "The best Kreisleriana to date," BILLBOARD. (Playing time 55 mins.) HCR 5204 **$2.00**

CATALOGUE OF DOVER BOOKS

SCHUMANN: TRIOS #1 IN D MINOR (OPUS 63) AND #3 IN G MINOR (OPUS 110), Trio di Bolzano. The fiery, romantic, melodic Trio #1 and the dramatic, seldom heard Trio #3 are both movingly played by a fine chamber ensemble. No one personified Romanticism to the general public of the 1840's more than did Robert Schumann, and among his most romantic works are these trios for cello, violin and piano. "Ensemble and overall interpretation leave little to be desired," HIGH FIDELITY. "An especially understanding performance," REV. OF RECORDED MUSIC. (Playing time 54 mins.) HCR 5205 **$2.00**

SCHUBERT: QUINTET IN A ("TROUT") (OPUS 114), AND NOCTURNE IN E FLAT (OPUS 148), Friedrich Wührer, Piano and Barchet Quartet. If there is a single piece of chamber music that is a universal favorite, it is probably Schubert's "Trout" Quintet. Delightful melody, harmonic resources, musical exuberance are its characteristics. The Nocturne (played by Wührer, Barchet, and Reimann) is an exquisite piece with a deceptively simple theme and harmony. "The best Trout on the market—Wührer is a fine Viennese-style Schubertian, and his spirit infects the Barchets," ATLANTIC MONTHLY. "Exquisitely recorded," ETUDE. (Playing time 44 mins.) HCR 5206 **$2.00**

SCHUBERT: PIANO SONATAS IN C MINOR AND B (OPUS 147), Friedrich Wührer. Schubert's sonatas retain the structure of the classical form, but delight listeners with romantic freedom and a special melodic richness. The C Minor, one of the Three Grand Sonatas, is a product of the composer's maturity. The B Major was not published until 15 years after his death. "Remarkable interpretation, reproduction of the first rank," DISQUES. "A superb pianist for music like this, musicianship, sweep, power, and an ability to integrate Schubert's measures such as few pianists have had since Schnabel," Harold Schonberg. (Playing time 49 mins.) HCR 5207 **$2.00**

STRAVINSKY: VIOLIN CONCERTO IN D, Ivry Gitlis, Cologne Orchestra; DUO CONCERTANTE, Ivry Gitlis, Violin, Charlotte Zelka, Piano, Cologne Orchestra; JEU DE CARTES, Bamberg Symphony, under Hollreiser. Igor Stravinsky is probably the most important composer of this century, and these three works are among the most significant of his neoclassical period of the 30's. The Violin Concerto is one of the few modern classics. Jeu de Cartes, a ballet score, bubbles with gaiety, color and melodiousness. "Imaginatively played and beautifully recorded," E. T. Canby, HARPERS MAGAZINE. "Gitlis is excellent, Hollreiser beautifully worked out," HIGH FIDELITY. (Playing time 55 mins.) HCR 5208 **$2.00**

GEMINIANI: SIX CONCERTI GROSSI, OPUS 3, Helma Elsner, Harpsichord, Barchet Quartet, Pro Musica Orch. of Stuttgart, under Reinhardt. Francesco Geminiani (1687-1762) has been rediscovered in the same musical exploration that revealed Scarlatti, Vivaldi, and Corelli. In form he is more sophisticated than the earlier Italians, but his music delights modern listeners with its combination of contrapuntal techniques and the full harmonies and rich melodies charcteristic of Italian music. This is the only recording of the six 1733 concerti: D Major, B Flat Minor, E Minor, G Minor, E Minor (bis), and D Minor. "I warmly recommend it, spacious, magnificent, I enjoyed every bar," C. Cudworth, RECORD NEWS. "Works of real charm, recorded with understanding and style," ETUDE. (Playing time 52 mins.) HCR 5209 **$2.00**

MODERN PIANO SONATAS: BARTOK: SONATA FOR PIANO; BLOCH: SONATA FOR PIANO (1935); PROKOFIEV, PIANO SONATA #7 IN B FLAT ("STALINGRAD"); STRAVINSKY: PIANO SONATA (1924), István Nádas, Piano. Shows some of the major forces and directions in modern piano music: Stravinsky's crisp austerity; Bartok's fusion of Hungarian folk motives; incisive diverse rhythms, and driving power; Bloch's distinctive emotional vigor; Prokofiev's brilliance and melodic beauty couched in pre-Romantic forms. "A most interesting documentation of the contemporary piano sonata. Nadas is a very good pianist." HIGH FIDELITY. (Playing time 59 mins.) HCR 5215 **$2.00**

VIVALDI: CONCERTI FOR FLUTE, VIOLIN, BASSOON, AND HARPSICHORD: #8 IN G MINOR, #21 IN F, #27 IN D, #7 IN D; SONATA #1 IN A MINOR, Gastone Tassinari, Renato Giangrandi, Giorgio Semprini, Arlette Eggmann. More than any other Baroque composer, Vivaldi moved the concerto grosso closer to the solo concert we deem standard today. In these concerti he wrote virtuosi music for the solo instruments, allowing each to introduce new material or expand on musical ideas, creating tone colors unusual even for Vivaldi. As a result, this record displays a new area of his genius, offering some of his most brilliant music. Performed by a top-rank European group. (Playing time 45 mins.) HCR 5216 **$2.00**

LÜBECK: CANTATAS: HILF DEINEM VOLK; GOTT, WIE DEIN NAME, Stuttgart Choral Society, Swabian Symphony Orch.; PRELUDES AND FUGUES IN C MINOR AND IN E, Eva Hölderlin, Organ. Vincent Lübeck (1654-1740), contemporary of Bach and Buxtehude, was one of the great figures of the 18th-century North German school. These examples of Lübeck's few surviving works indicate his power and brilliance. Voice and instrument lines in the cantatas are strongly reminiscent of the organ: the preludes and fugues show the influence of Bach and Buxtehude. This is the only recording of the superb cantatas. Text and translation included. "Outstanding record," E. T. Canby, SAT. REVIEW. "Hölderlin's playing is exceptional," AM. RECORD REVIEW. "Will make [Lübeck] many new friends," Philip Miller. (Playing time 37 mins.) HCR 5217 **$2.00**

CATALOGUE OF DOVER BOOKS

DONIZETTI, BETLY (LA CAPANNA SVIZZERA), Soloists of Compagnia del Teatro dell'Opera Comica di Roma, Societa del Quartetto, Rome, Chorus and Orch. Betly, a delightful one-act opera written in 1836, is similar in style and story to one of Donizetti's better-known operas, L'Elisir. Betly is lighthearted and farcical, with bright melodies and a freshness characteristic of the best of Donizetti. Libretto (English and Italian) included. "The chief honors go to Angela Tuccari who sings the title role, and the record is worth having for her alone," M. Rayment, GRAMOPHONE REC. REVIEW. "The interpretation . . . is excellent . . . This is a charming record which we recommend to lovers of little-known works," DISQUES.
HCR 5218 **$2.00**

ROSSINI: L'OCCASIONE FA IL LADRO (IL CAMBIO DELLA VALIGIA), Soloists of Compagnia del Teatro dell'Opera Comica di Roma, Societa del Quartetto, Rome, Chorus and Orch. A charming one-act opera buffa, this is one of the first works of Rossini's maturity, and it is filled with the wit, gaiety and sparkle that make his comic operas second only to Mozart's. Like other Rossini works, L'Occasione makes use of the theme of impersonation and attendant amusing confusions. This is the only recording of this important buffa. Full libretto (English and Italian) included. "A major rebirth, a stylish performance . . . the Roman recording engineers have outdone themselves," H. Weinstock, SAT. REVIEW. (Playing time 53 mins.)
HCR 5219 **$2.00**

DOWLAND: "FIRST BOOKE OF AYRES," Pro Musica Antiqua of Brussels, Safford Cape, Director. This is the first recording to include all 22 of the songs of this great collection, written by John Dowland, one of the most important writers of songs of 16th and 17th century England. The participation of the Brussels Pro Musica under Safford Cape insures scholarly accuracy and musical artistry. "Powerfully expressive and very beautiful," B. Haggin. "The musicianly singers . . . never fall below an impressive standard," Philip Miller. Text included. (Playing time 51 mins.)
HCR 5220 **$2.00**

FRENCH CHANSONS AND DANCES OF THE 16TH CENTURY, Pro Musica Antiqua of Brussels, Safford Cape, Director. A remarkable selection of 26 three- or four-part chansons and delightful dances from the French Golden Age—by such composers as Orlando Lasso, Crecquillon, Claude Gervaise, etc. Text and translation included. "Delightful, well-varied with respect to mood and to vocal and instrumental color," HIGH FIDELITY. "Performed with . . . discrimination and musical taste, full of melodic distinction and harmonic resource," Irving Kolodin. (Playing time 39 mins.)
HCR 5221 **$2.00**

GALUPPI: CONCERTI A QUATRO: #1 IN G MINOR, #2 IN G, #3 IN D, #4 IN C MINOR, #5 IN E FLAT, AND #6 IN B FLAT, Biffoli Quartet. During Baldassare Galuppi's lifetime, his instrumental music was widely renowned, and his contemporaries Mozart and Haydn thought highly of his work. These 6 concerti reflect his great ability; and they are among the most interesting compositions of the period. They are remarkable for their unusual combinations of timbres and for emotional elements that were only then beginning to be introduced in music. Performed by the well-known Biffoli Quartet, this is the only record devoted exclusively to Galuppi. (Playing time 47 mins.)
HCR 5222 **$2.00**

HAYDN: DIVERTIMENTI FOR WIND BAND, IN C; IN F; DIVERTIMENTO A NOVE STROMENTI IN C FOR STRINGS AND WIND INSTRUMENTS, reconstructed by H. C. Robbins Landon, performed by members of Vienna State Opera Orch.; MOZART DIVERTIMENTI IN C, III (K. 187) AND IV (K. 188), Salzburg Wind Ensemble. Robbins Landon discovered Haydn manuscripts in a Benedictine monastery in Lower Austria, edited them and restored their original instrumentation The result is this magnificent record. Two little-known divertimenti by Mozart—of great charm and appeal—are also included. None of this music is available elsewhere (Playing time 58 mins.)
HCR 5223 **$2.00**

PURCELL: TRIO SONATAS FROM "SONATAS OF FOUR PARTS" (1697): #9 IN F ("GOLDEN"), #7 IN C, #1 IN B MINOR, #10 IN D, #4 IN D MINOR, #2 IN E FLAT, AND #8 IN G MINOR, Giorgio Ciompi, and Werner Torkanowsky, Violins, Geo. Koutzen, Cello, and Herman Chessid, Harpsichord. These posthumously-published sonatas show Purcell at his most advanced and mature. They are certainly among the finest musical examples of pre-modern chamber music. Those not familiar with his instrumental music are well-advised to hear these outstanding pieces. "Performance sounds excellent," Harold Schonberg. "Some of the most noble and touching music known to anyone," AMERICAN RECORD GUIDE. (Playing time 58 mins.)
HCR 5224 **$2.00**

BARTOK: VIOLIN CONCERTO; SONATA FOR UNACCOMPANIED VIOLIN, Ivry Gitlis, Pro Musica of Vienna, under Hornstein. Both these works are outstanding examples of Bartok's final period, and they show his powers at their fullest. The Violin Concerto is, in the opinion of many authorities, Bartok's finest work, and the Sonata, his last work, is "a masterpiece" (F. Sackville West). "Wonderful, finest performance of both Bartok works I have ever heard," GRAMOPHONE. "Gitlis has such potent and musical sense out of these two works that I suspect many general music lovers (not otherwise in sympathy with modern music) will discover to their amazement that they like it. Exceptionally good sound," AUDITOR. (Playing time 54 mins.)
HCR 5211 **$2.00**

Language Books and Records

GERMAN: HOW TO SPEAK AND WRITE IT. AN INFORMAL CONVERSATIONAL METHOD FOR SELF STUDY, Joseph Rosenberg. Eminently useful for self study because of concentration on elementary stages of learning. Also provides teachers with remarkable variety of aids: 28 full- and double-page sketches with pertinent items numbered and identified in German and English; German proverbs, jokes; grammar, idiom studies; extensive practice exercises. The most interesting introduction to German available, full of amusing illustrations, photographs of cities and landmarks in German-speaking cities, cultural information subtly woven into conversational material. Includes summary of grammar, guide to letter writing, study guide to German literature by Dr. Richard Friedenthal. Index. 400 illustrations. 384pp. 5⅜ x 8½.
T271 Paperbound **$2.00**

FRENCH: HOW TO SPEAK AND WRITE IT. AN INFORMAL CONVERSATIONAL METHOD FOR SELF STUDY, Joseph Lemaitre. Even the absolute beginner can acquire a solid foundation for further study from this delightful elementary course. Photographs, sketches and drawings, sparkling colloquial conversations on a wide variety of topics (including French culture and custom), French sayings and quips, are some of aids used to demonstrate rather than merely describe the language. Thorough yet surprisingly entertaining approach, excellent for teaching and for self study. Comprehensive analysis of pronunciation, practice exercises and appendices of verb tables, additional vocabulary, other useful material. Index. Appendix. 400 illustrations. 416pp. 5⅜ x 8½.
T268 Paperbound **$2.00**

DICTIONARY OF SPOKEN SPANISH, Spanish-English, English-Spanish. Compiled from spoken Spanish, emphasizing idiom and colloquial usage in both Castilian and Latin-American. More than 16,000 entries containing over 25,000 idioms—the largest list of idiomatic constructions ever published. Complete sentences given, indexed under single words—language in immediately useable form, for travellers, businessmen, students, etc. 25 page introduction provides rapid survey of sounds, grammar, syntax, with full consideration of irregular verbs. Especially apt in modern treatment of phrases and structure. 17 page glossary gives translations of geographical names, money values, numbers, national holidays, important street signs, useful expressions of high frequency, plus unique 7 page glossary of Spanish and Spanish-American foods and dishes. Originally published as War Department Technical Manual TM 30-900. iv + 513pp. 5⅜ x 8.
T495 Paperbound **$1.75**

SPEAK MY LANGUAGE: SPANISH FOR YOUNG BEGINNERS, M. Ahlman, Z. Gilbert. Records provide one of the best, and most entertaining, methods of introducing a foreign language to children. Within the framework of a train trip from Portugal to Spain, an English-speaking child is introduced to Spanish by a native companion. (Adapted from a successful radio program of the N. Y. State Educational Department.) Though a continuous story, there are a dozen specific categories of expressions, including greetings, numbers, time, weather, food, clothes, family members, etc. Drill is combined with poetry and contextual use. Authentic background music is heard. An accompanying book enables a reader to follow the records, and includes a vocabulary of over 350 recorded expressions. Two 10″ 33⅓ records, total of 40 minutes. Book. 40 illustrations. 69pp. 5¼ x 10½.
T890 The set **$4.95**

AN ENGLISH-FRENCH-GERMAN-SPANISH WORD FREQUENCY DICTIONARY, H. S. Eaton. An indispensable language study aid, this is a semantic frequency list of the 6000 most frequently used words in 4 languages—24,000 words in all. The lists, based on concepts rather than words alone, and containing all modern, exact, and idiomatic vocabulary, are arranged side by side to form a unique 4-language dictionary. A simple key indicates the importance of the individual words within each language. Over 200 pages of separate indexes for each language enable you to locate individual words at a glance. Will help language teachers and students, authors of textbooks, grammars, and language tests to compare concepts in the various languages and to concentrate on basic vocabulary, avoiding uncommon and obsolete words. 2 Appendixes. xxi + 441pp. 6½ x 9¼.
T738 Paperbound **$2.45**

NEW RUSSIAN-ENGLISH AND ENGLISH-RUSSIAN DICTIONARY, M. A. O'Brien. Over 70,000 entries in the new orthography! Many idiomatic uses and colloquialisms which form the basis of actual speech. Irregular verbs, perfective and imperfective aspects, regular and irregular sound changes, and other features. One of the few dictionaries where accent changes within the conjugation of verbs and the declension of nouns are fully indicated. "One of the best," Prof. E. J. Simmons, Cornell. First names, geographical terms, bibliography, etc. 738pp. 4½ x 6¼.
T208 Paperbound **$2.00**

96 MOST USEFUL PHRASES FOR TOURISTS AND STUDENTS in English, French, Spanish, German, Italian. A handy folder you'll want to carry with you. How to say "Excuse me," "How much is it?", "Write it down, please," etc., in four foreign languages. Copies limited, no more than 1 to a customer. **FREE**

CATALOGUE OF DOVER BOOKS

Say It language phrase books

These handy phrase books (128 to 196 pages each) make grammatical drills unnecessary for an elementary knowledge of a spoken foreign language. Covering most matters of travel and everyday life each volume contains:

Over 1000 phrases and sentences in immediately useful forms — foreign language plus English.

Modern usage designed for Americans. Specific phrases like, "Give me small change," and "Please call a taxi."

Simplified phonetic transcription you will be able to read at sight.

The only completely indexed phrase books on the market.

Covers scores of important situations: — Greetings, restaurants, sightseeing, useful expressions, etc.

These books are prepared by native linguists who are professors at Columbia, N.Y.U., Fordham and other great universities. Use them independently or with any other book or record course. They provide a supplementary living element that most other courses lack. Individual volumes in:

Russian 75¢	Italian 75¢	Spanish 75¢	German 75¢
Hebrew 75¢	Danish 75¢	Japanese 75¢	Swedish 75¢
Dutch 75¢	Esperanto 75¢	Modern Greek 75¢	Portuguese 75¢
Norwegian 75¢	Polish 75¢	French 75¢	Yiddish 75¢
Turkish 75¢		English for German-speaking people 75¢	
English for Italian-speaking people 75¢		English for Spanish-speaking people 75¢	

Large clear type. 128-196 pages each. 3½ x 5¼. Sturdy paper binding.

Listen and Learn language records

LISTEN & LEARN is the only language record course designed especially to meet your travel and everyday needs. It is available in separate sets for FRENCH, SPANISH, GERMAN, JAPANESE, RUSSIAN, MODERN GREEK, PORTUGUESE, ITALIAN and HEBREW, and each set contains three 33⅓ rpm long-playing records—1½ hours of recorded speech by eminent native speakers who are professors at Columbia, New York University, Queens College.

Check the following special features found only in LISTEN & LEARN:

● **Dual-language recording. 812 selected phrases and sentences, over 3200 words,** spoken first in English, then in their foreign language equivalents. A suitable pause follows each foreign phrase, allowing you time to repeat the expression. You learn by unconscious assimilation.

● **128 to 206-page manual** contains everything on the records, plus a simple phonetic pronunciation guide.

● **Indexed for convenience. The only set on the market** that is completely indexed. No more puzzling over where to find the phrase you need. Just look in the rear of the manual.

● **Practical.** No time wasted on material you can find in any grammar. LISTEN & LEARN covers central core material with phrase approach. Ideal for the person with limited learning time.

● **Living, modern expressions,** not found in other courses. Hygienic products, modern equipment, shopping—expressions used every day, like "nylon" and "air-conditioned."

● **Limited objective.** Everything you learn, no matter where you stop, is immediately useful. You have to finish other courses, wade through grammar and vocabulary drill, before they help you.

● **High-fidelity recording.** LISTEN & LEARN records equal in clarity and surface-silence any record on the market costing up to $6.

"Excellent . . . the spoken records . . . impress me as being among the very best on the market," **Prof. Mario Pei,** Dept. of Romance Languages, Columbia University. "Inexpensive and well-done . . . it would make an ideal present," CHICAGO SUNDAY TRIBUNE. "More genuinely helpful than anything of its kind which I have previously encountered," **Sidney Clark,** well-known author of "ALL THE BEST" travel books.

UNCONDITIONAL GUARANTEE. Try LISTEN & LEARN, then return it within 10 days for full refund if you are not satisfied.

Each set contains three twelve-inch 33⅓ records, manual, and album.

SPANISH	the set $5.95	GERMAN		the set $5.95
FRENCH	the set $5.95	ITALIAN		the set $5.95
RUSSIAN	the set $5.95	JAPANESE		the set $5.95
PORTUGUESE	the set $5.95	MODERN GREEK		the set $5.95
MODERN HEBREW	the set $5.95			

Trubner Colloquial Manuals

These unusual books are members of the famous Trubner series of colloquial manuals. They have been written to provide adults with a sound colloquial knowledge of a foreign language, and are suited for either class use or self-study. Each book is a complete course in itself, with progressive, easy to follow lessons. Phonetics, grammar, and syntax are covered, while hundreds of phrases and idioms, reading texts, exercises, and vocabulary are included. These books are unusual in being neither skimpy nor overdetailed in grammatical matters, and in presenting up-to-date, colloquial, and practical phrase material. Bilingual presentation is stressed, to make thorough self-study easier for the reader.

COLLOQUIAL HINDUSTANI, A. H. Harley, formerly Nizam's Reader in Urdu, U. of London. 30 pages on phonetics and scripts (devanagari & Arabic-Persian) are followed by 29 lessons, including material on English and Arabic-Persian influences. Key to all exercises. Vocabulary. 5 x 7½. 147pp. Clothbound **$1.75**

COLLOQUIAL PERSIAN, L. P. Elwell-Sutton. Best introduction to modern Persian, with 90 page grammatical section followed by conversations, 35-page vocabulary. 139pp.
Clothbound **$1.75**

COLLOQUIAL ARABIC, DeLacy O'Leary. Foremost Islamic scholar covers language of Egypt, Syria, Palestine, & Northern Arabia. Extremely clear coverage of complex Arabic verbs & noun plurals; also cultural aspects of language. Vocabulary. xviii + 192pp. 5 x 7½.
Clothbound **$2.50**

COLLOQUIAL GERMAN, P. F. Doring. Intensive thorough coverage of grammar in easily-followed form. Excellent for brush-up, with hundreds of colloquial phrases. 34 pages of bilingual texts. 224pp. 5 x 7½. Clothbound **$1.75**

COLLOQUIAL SPANISH, W. R. Patterson. Castilian grammar and colloquial language, loaded with bilingual phrases and colloquialisms. Excellent for review or self-study. 164pp. 5 x 7½.
Clothbound **$1.75**

COLLOQUIAL FRENCH, W. R. Patterson. 16th revision of this extremely popular manual. Grammar explained with model clarity, and hundreds of useful expressions and phrases; exercises, reading texts, etc. Appendixes of new and useful words and phrases. 223pp. 5 x 7½.
Clothbound **$1.75**

COLLOQUIAL CZECH, J. Schwarz, former headmaster of Lingua Institute, Prague. Full easily followed coverage of grammar, hundreds of immediately useable phrases, texts. Perhaps the best Czech grammar in print. "An absolutely successful textbook," JOURNAL OF CZECHO-SLOVAK FORCES IN GREAT BRITAIN. 252pp. 5 x 7½. Clothbound **$3.00**

COLLOQUIAL RUMANIAN, G. Nandris, Professor of University of London. Extremely thorough coverage of phonetics, grammar, syntax; also included 70-page reader, and 70-page vocabulary. Probably the best grammar for this increasingly important language. 340pp. 5 x 7½.
Clothbound **$2.50**

COLLOQUIAL ITALIAN, A. L. Hayward. Excellent self-study course in grammar, vocabulary, idioms, and reading. Easy progressive lessons will give a good working knowledge of Italian in the shortest possible time. 5 x 7½. Clothbound **$1.75**

COLLOQUIAL TURKISH, Yusuf Mardin. Very clear, thorough introduction to leading cultural and economic language of Near East. Begins with pronunciation and statement of vowel harmony, then 36 lessons present grammar, graded vocabulary, useful phrases, dialogues, reading, exercises. Key to exercises at rear. Turkish-English vocabulary. All in Roman alphabet. x + 288pp. 4¾ x 7¼. Clothbound **$4.00**

DUTCH-ENGLISH AND ENGLISH-DUTCH DICTIONARY, F. G. Renier. For travel, literary, scientific or business Dutch, you will find this the most convenient, practical and comprehensive dictionary on the market. More than 60,000 entries, shades of meaning, colloquialisms, idioms, compounds and technical terms. Dutch and English strong and irregular verbs. This is the only dictionary in its size and price range that indicates the gender of nouns. New orthography. xvii + 571pp. 5½ x 6¼. T224 Clothbound **$2.75**

LEARN DUTCH, F. G. Renier. This book is the most satisfactory and most easily used grammar of modern Dutch. The student is gradually led from simple lessons in pronunciation, through translation from and into Dutch, and finally to a mastery of spoken and written Dutch. Grammatical principles are clearly explained while a useful, practical vocabulary is introduced in easy exercises and readings. It is used and recommended by the Fulbright Committee in the Netherlands. Phonetic appendices. Over 1200 exercises; Dutch-English, English-Dutch vocabularies. 181pp. 4¼ x 7¼. T441 Clothbound **$2.25**

Orientalia

ORIENTAL RELIGIONS IN ROMAN PAGANISM, F. Cumont. A study of the cultural meeting of east and west in the Early Roman Empire. It covers the most important eastern religions of the time from their first appearance in Rome, 204 B.C., when the Great Mother of the Gods was first brought over from Syria. The ecstatic cults of Syria and Phrygia — Cybele, Attis, Adonis, their orgies and mutilatory rites; the mysteries of Egypt — Serapis, Isis, Osiris, the dualism of Persia, the elevation of cosmic evil to equal stature with the deity, Mithra; worship of Hermes Trismegistus; Ishtar, Astarte; the magic of the ancient Near East, etc. Introduction. 55pp. of notes; extensive bibliography. Index. xxiv + 298pp. 5⅜ x 8.
T321 Paperbound **$1.75**

THE MYSTERIES OF MITHRA, F. Cumont. The definitive coverage of a great ideological struggle between the west and the orient in the first centuries of the Christian era. The origin of Mithraism, a Persian mystery religion, and its association with the Roman army is discussed in detail. Then utilizing fragmentary monuments and texts, in one of the greatest feats of scholarly detection, Dr. Cumont reconstructs the mystery teachings and secret doctrines, the hidden organization and cult of Mithra. Mithraic art is discussed, analyzed, and depicted in 70 illustrations. 239pp. 5⅜ x 8.
T323 Paperbound **$1.85**

CHRISTIAN AND ORIENTAL PHILOSOPHY OF ART, A. K. Coomaraswamy. A unique fusion of philosopher, orientalist, art historian, and linguist, the author discusses such matters as: the true function of aesthetics in art, the importance of symbolism, intellectual and philosophic backgrounds, the role of traditional culture in enriching art, common factors in all great art, the nature of medieval art, the nature of folklore, the beauty of mathematics, and similar topics. 2 illustrations. Bibliography. 148pp. 5⅜ x 8.
T378 Paperbound **$1.25**

TRANSFORMATION OF NATURE IN ART, A. K. Coomaraswamy. Unabridged reissue of a basic work upon Asiatic religious art and philosophy of religion. The theory of religious art in Asia and Medieval Europe (exemplified by Meister Eckhart) is analyzed and developed. Detailed consideration is given to Indian medieval aesthetic manuals, symbolic language in philosophy, the origin and use of images in India, and many other fascinating and little known topics. Glossaries of Sanskrit and Chinese terms. Bibliography. 41pp. of notes. 245pp. 5⅜ x 8.
T368 Paperbound **$1.75**

BUDDHIST LOGIC, F.Th. Stcherbatsky. A study of an important part of Buddhism usually ignored by other books on the subject: the Mahayana buddhistic logic of the school of Dignaga and his followers. First vol. devoted to history of Indian logic with Central Asian continuations, detailed exposition of Dignaga system, including theory of knowledge, the sensible world (causation, perception, ultimate reality) and mental world (judgment, inference, logical fallacies, the syllogism), reality of external world, and negation (law of contradiction, universals, dialectic). Vol. II contains translation of Dharmakirti's Nyayabindu with Dharmamottara's commentary. Appendices cover translations of Tibetan treatises on logic, Hindu attacks on Buddhist logic, etc. The basic work, one of the products of the great St. Petersburg school of Indian studies. Written clearly and with an awareness of Western philosophy and logic; meant for the Asian specialist and for the general reader with only a minimum of background. Vol. I, xii + 559pp. Vol. II, viii + 468pp. 5⅜ x 8½.
T955 Vol. I Paperbound **$2.35**
T956 Vol. II Paperbound **$2.35**
The set **$4.70**

THE TEXTS OF TAOISM. The first inexpensive edition of the complete James Legge translations of the Tao Te King and the writings of Chinese mystic Chuang Tse. Also contains several shorter treatises: the T'ai Shang Tractate of Actions and Their Retributions; the King Kang King, or Classic of Purity; the Yin Fu King, or Classic of the Harmony of the Seen and Unseen; the Yu Shu King, or Classic of the Pivot of Jade; and the Hsia Yung King, or Classic of the Directory for a Day. While there are other translations of the Tao Te King, this is the only translation of Chuang Tse and much of other material. Extensive introduction discusses differences between Taoism, Buddhism, Confucianism; authenticity and arrangement of Tao Te King and writings of Chuang Tse; the meaning of the Tao and basic tenets of Taoism; historical accounts of Lao-tse and followers; other pertinent matters. Clarifying notes incorporated into text. Originally published as Volumes 39, 40 of SACRED BOOKS OF THE EAST series, this has long been recognized as an indispensible collection. Sinologists, philosophers, historians of religion of course be interested and anyone with an elementary course in Oriental religion or philosophy will understand and profit from these writings. Index. Appendix analyzing thought of Chuang Tse. Vol. I, xxiii + 396pp. Vol. II, viii + 340pp. 5⅜ x 8½.
T990 Vol. I Paperbound **$2.00**
T991 Vol. II Paperbound **$2.00**

CATALOGUE OF DOVER BOOKS

EPOCHS OF CHINESE AND JAPANESE ART, Ernest T. Fenollosa. Although this classic of art history was written before the archeological discovery of Shang and Chou civilizations, it is still in many respects the finest detailed study of Chinese and Japanese art available in English. It is very wide in range, covering sculpture, carving, painting, metal work, ceramics, textiles, graphic arts and other areas, and it considers both religious and secular art, including the Japanese woodcut. Its greatest strength, however, lies in its extremely full, detailed, insight-laden discussion of historical and cultural background, and in its analysis of the religious and philosophical implications of art works. It is also a brilliant stylistic achievement, written with enthusiasm and verve, which can be enjoyed and read with profit by both the Orientalist and the general reader who is interested in art. Index. Glossary of proper names. 242 illustrations. Total of 704 pages. 5⅜ x 8½.

T364-5 Two vol. set, paperbound **$5.00**

THE VEDANTA SUTRAS OF BADARAYANA WITH COMMENTARY BY SANKARACHARYA. The definitive translation of the consummation, foremost interpretation of Upanishads. Originally part of SACRED BOOKS OF THE EAST, this two-volume translation includes exhaustive commentary and exegesis by Sankara; 128-page introduction by translator, Prof. Thibaut, that discusses background, scope and purpose of the sutras, value and importance of Sankara's interpretation; copious footnotes providing further explanations. Every serious student of Indian religion or thought, philosophers, historians of religion should read these clear, accurate translations of documents central to development of important thought systems in the East. Unabridged republication of Volumes 34, 38 of the Sacred Books of the East. Translated by George Thibault. General index, index of quotations and of Sanskrit. Vol. I, cxxv + 448pp. Vol. II, iv + 506pp. 5⅜ x 8½.

T994 Vol. I Paperbound **$2.00**
T995 Vol. II Paperbound **$2.00**

THE UPANISHADS. The Max Müller translation of the twelve classical Upanishads available for the first time in an inexpensive format: Chandogya, Kena, Aitareya aranyaka and upanishad, Kaushitaki, Isa, Katha, Mundaka, Taittiriyaka Brhadaranyaka, Svetarasvatara. Prasna — all of the classical Upanishads of the Vedanta school—and the Maitriyana Upanishad. Originally volumes 1, 15 of SACRED BOOKS OF THE EAST series, this is still the most scholarly translation. Prof. Müller, probably most important Sanskritologist of nineteenth century, provided invaluable introduction that acquaints readers with history of Upanishad translations, age and chronology of texts, etc. and a preface that discusses their value to Western readers. Heavily annotated. Stimulating reading for anyone with even only a basic course background in Oriental philosophy, religion, necessary to all Indologists, philosophers, religious historians. Transliteration and pronunciation guide. Vol. I, ciii + 320pp. Vol. II, liii + 350pp.

T992 Vol. I Paperbound **$2.00**
T993 Vol. II Paperbound **$2.00**
The set **$4.00**

Dover publishes books on art, music, philosophy, literature, languages, history, social sciences, psychology, handcrafts, orientalia, puzzles and entertainments, chess, pets and gardens, books explaining science, intermediate and higher mathematics, mathematical physics, engineering, biological sciences, earth sciences, classics of science, etc. Write to:

Dept. catrr.
Dover Publications, Inc.
180 Varick Street, N. Y. 14, N. Y.